التعليمات بالداخل
INSTRUCTIONS WITHIN

ASHRAF FAYADH
أشرف فياض

TRANS. MONA KAREEM
WITH MONA ZAKI AND JONATHAN WRIGHT

ED. AMMIEL ALCALAY, PIERRE JORIS,
AND LYNNE DESILVA-JOHNSON

التعليمات بالداخل
INSTRUCTIONS WITHIN

ISBN 978-0-9860505-7-2
Library of Congress Control Number 2016911110

copyright © 2016 by Ashraf Fayadh
with original paintings on front and back cover
by Ashraf Fayadh
poetry translated by Mona Kareem,
with additional translation by
Mona Zaki and Jonathan Wright
edited and facilitated by Lynne DeSilva-Johnson,
with Ammiel Alcalay and Pierre Joris
Introduction by Mohammed Kheder

Cover design, book design and layout by Lynne DeSilva-Johnson

*This text was set in Adobe Arabic, Sana, Eid Al Fitr-I, Minion Pro, and OCR-A Standard,
printed and bound by Spencer Printing and Graphics in Honesdale, PA, in the USA,
and distributed to the trade by Small Press Distribution / SPD.*

THE OPERATING SYSTEM//PRESS
141 Spencer Street #203
Brooklyn, NY 11205

التعليمات بالداخل

INSTRUCTIONS WITHIN

ACKNOWLEGEMENTS AND THANKS

This book is the work of many hands,
and the result of many hearts
in many countries
not only willing but *wanting*,
seeking to give time, energy, words, and self
without compensation
in the service of Ashraf's poetry and art
and
in the service of justice for his person.

My gratitude knows no bounds
and faith in the good in people
is restored in your deeds.

To our team of transcribers:
Mohamad, Khaled, Farah, Kamella,
Nour, Hassan and Mowafak;
to Ammiel, Margaret, and Pierre;
to Abdellatif Laabi and Tahar Ben Jelloun;
to Mona Zaki and Jonathan Wright;
to Mohamed Kheder;
to Ahmed Mater
and
to all the artists, poets, musicians,
bloggers, teachers, and others
who shared, spoke, made, taught and fought
to assure no sentence could silence this voice.

You deserve so much more, but simply: thank you.

- Lynne DeSilva-Johnson -
founder and editor, The Operating System

ADVANCE PRAISE FOR INSTRUCTIONS WITHIN

Why do you need to read this book in America today?

Because a US journalist asked if it really was worth it to write poems that might get you killed.

Because Ashraf Fayadh, as poet, artist and human being, is being jailed and tortured for doing his job, that is for daring to expose & deride the two-headed Moloch governing the country he lives in (Saudi Arabia) and ours (these States): Fundamentalist religion & oil-money.

Because Ashraf Fayadh is inventing a needed poetics to break not only those taboos but also the shackles of standard Arab poetics, freeing the language — & a freed language is needed for free thinking.

Because his own exile (he is of Palestinian extraction) is so absolute that it does not fit the traditional nostalgic poetics of exile & searches for a new way of saying a new & wilder dislocation.

Because this exile is so close to all of our own dislocations, even as, smugly ensconced in our North American bunker, we don't see that the same future is awaiting us.

Because he wrote: "I am Hell's experiment on planet Earth."

Pierre Joris

This sentence teaches us all we need to know about Ashraf Fayadh's poetry — about his strength, about his violence.

Poets are rebels, bearers of fire, companions of truth and fact. They are the light that extinguishes shadows and gives words to things that die if they are not said. They are fragile and strong at the same time. They possess only their breath and a soul that resists. You can beat them, whip them, throw them into the bottom of wells, bury them alive, their voice continues to rise and wake up the world.

Tribunals detest them. States fear them. The law pursues and prosecutes them. Religions distrust and denounce them. But it is the poets who give the earth its salt, its grain of madness, its music and songs. Poetry can only be searing, brilliant, skeptical, restless. It has a pact with eternity. One remembers the poets, never their judges. Al-Hallaj, the great mystical poet, was executed in 922 in Baghdad for his excessive love of God. But his poetry is still on the lips of all the generations.

Poetry will not give up its weapons, the words and images that it invents. You cannot shoot it. Like freedom, like the values that found a civilization, you cannot eradicate it by cutting off the head of a man because his words don't please the powerful—these types without conscience or humanity.

Tahar Ben Jelloun

My dear Ashraf,

I'd like to begin this letter, not the usual way this time, with a quote: "Courage is a matter of organization," as André Malraux used to say. Why is that? You know that I myself was imprisoned for many years and, at one point during that experience, my life was in danger. So I can put myself in your place more than just a bit, guess what your spirit is undergoing, your heart and your guts, imagine just how you've collected yourself so that courage won't desert you.

On this last point, I know, we know, that you have an asset of the first order: poetry, which I would not hesitate to define as a school of courage. And real courage does not reside in what this school teaches us to practice: is it not more the truth about oneself, whatever it costs, the refusal of whatever consensus exists, independence in the face of the powers that be, going head to head with the language in which one expresses oneself, and fidelity to the word given in what one writes?

Having read your Instructions within first in Arabic and then more intimately while translating it into French, I had the conviction that you have honored perfectly the exigencies of this teaching and integrated the principles of its ethic. And this is what surely permits you to hold your head high in your cell, I say, unto the stars. To keep, even in the black night, your eyes open to the interior within yourself, and also fully to the exterior, to the human condition.

You know Ashraf, I've come up with a crazy idea, extravagant even, but I think that, in countries where the arbitrary reigns, where liberty is scorned, where human dignity is trampled, then the poet's true place is… in prison! This bastion, this "citadel of exile" is, in a sense, the best place from which to denounce a regime that oppresses its people. In fact, it is the regime that denounces itself, and in the most eloquent way possible, by putting the poet in prison.

Well then, let's return to things more sensible and eminently more desirable! It is your complete and full liberty that we, thousands of poets and hundreds of thousands of citizens throughout the world, are calling for. Yes, let's keep building that dream, there, and believe in it, hard like iron. And together, keep to hope.

I embrace you.
Like a brother

It must be said that poets are not the only victims of intolerance and despotism. The recent beheadings of dozens in that country prove this. But through the simple fact of practicing their art, poets are among the most exposed to the vindictiveness of the authorities because they are free spirits whose word is itself a counter-power. From its very origins until the present, Arabic poetry has included a great number of free and audacious spirits. We need only cite the example of Abu Nuwas (8th c.), with his celebration of wine and love, including that of young acolytes. Two centuries later Abu-al-Ala al-Ma'arri was a declared agnostic, dismissing all religions, one after another, with pessimism and sarcasm. While fully inscribing himself into this tradition, Ashraf Fayadh is a contemporary poet who speaks to the world that is ours with words and images of a grand modernity. A satirical poet, he rails at society, but not only the one in which he lives where oil has become god and its price on the stock market determines the life and death of his country and its people. Yet, he is also a poet of intimacy, struggling against his demons in quest of his own human truth.

Abdellatif Laabi

Palestinian poet, artist and cultural activist Ashraf Fayadh reminds us, through his life and work, that blasphemy (for which he has been sentenced to 8 years in prison and 800 lashes) is still a crime in Saudi Arabia, but also that poetry is powerful against the criminal madness of a deranged state: ". . . these pages have exhausted all languages known to earth / . . . to offer a name that matches your definition of self / your name—

like an inkwell pregnant with possibilities." The Operating System does us an extraordinary service by making this magnificent poet's voice available. Read Fayadh to understand what we are fighting against, and for!"

Margaret Randall

Just a few years before his death, the great poet Amiri Baraka railed against what he saw as a poetry of complacency, of "the indoors," and harkened back to those of his generation (and older), "who actually worked to register some understanding of 'the great outdoors' i.e., the real world." It is with more than some irony that we here, in the belly of the imperial beast, must seek such poetry of "the great outdoors" from someone like Ashraf Fayadh, a Palestinian imprisoned in Saudi Arabia. Like the real world, Fayadh's poems are dizzying in their associations and resonance, recalling echoes of lines from different times, languages, and circumstances, from revery to exile, from brutality to utmost tenderness. Poet and artist Etel Adnan once wrote that "Palestine is a land planted / by eyes refusing to be closed." The poetry of Ashraf Fayadh, in a dream state of vigilance, attention, and horror, forces us to look at the world we actually inhabit, in all its glory and horror.

Ammiel Alcalay

Translations of Laabi and Ben Jelloun by Ammiel Alcalay & Miriam Nichols

FOREWARD

It was 2003 when I met Ashraf Fayadh. I first knew him as an artist showcasing his works at the galleries of Abha city. With him, I got to discover more about contemporary art and its unique vision of the world. Later, I read his first poetry collection Instructions Within, a book that stood out at the time for its aesthetic difference and ability to employ what others label as "unpoetic" such as exile, home, dreams, and other human questions charged with melancholy, despair, sarcasm, and pain. The alienation he felt was not permanent; whether in his poetry or life. He kept these important questions grow with him, around home and Gaza and a life of unexpected troubles. In poetry, his wonderings surpass the normal and redundant of political issues as he aims for a unique reading of today's world. He once told me that these big questions accompanied him since his childhood in Abha, especially when he entered elementary school and noticed how his classmates treated him "differently". He was sad but he overcame his trauma through poetry.

Poetry helped Ashraf reconcile with reality and memory, with his inner dialectic history. He never forgot the days he spent in Gaza and the memories of others surrounding him in diaspora. He also recalled these memories in joy and love; it might have provided him with the hope and consolation needed for daily survival. It was remedy for the troubles he had faced. Perhaps Ashraf's deep and fascinating faith in art helped him devote his time to bringing something valuable into the scene. He was against an art that would not relate to people's anxieties and realities. So he kept working and writing, producing texts and artworks that touch on fundamental questions such as existence, identity, and the current moment.

After meeting Ashraf, a group of us founded a creative collective which we named Shatta (various). We misspelled in the Arabic to give it that contemporary twist. There was a flaming desire at the time to do something different and challenging. Despite the worries and fears, we started to work, curating our first exhibition in Jeddah, after publishing a first declaration towards an art of the daily and the spatial. We let ourselves experiment, searching for a new humanism, making unfinished concepts, relying on coincidence and waste in artworks, establishing something out of void and performance, bridging a gap with a reader who had previously felt alienated by surrealism and abstract. It was a successful experience in breaking away from the classism and elitism of art. From pure aesthetics, which color life with joy, to a charged and troubled reality. We lifted art from the professional, skilled, and polished to the daily and surrounding, that enrich one's senses. We wanted to make art accessible.

This was one of several projects that brought me and Ashraf together, as we looked to reshape questions of the daily life. One example would be the identification cards which he had created for people based on their interests, preferences, and pleasures. And on a bandage, he drew a map of a world in bleeding. He has several poetry collections that haven't yet been published. Shortly before his arrest, he was starting to curate several exhibitions and projects. My friend Ashraf is now paying the cost. The cost of believing in the freedom of word, which triggered the men of darkness against him. They worked in all ways possible to stop him; from testifying against him to accusing him with fraud charges. Yet, he remains the candle of our poetry, with which we see more of the world.

Mohamed Kheder

TRANSLATORS' NOTES

When Ashraf Fayadh was arrested in 2014, I translated one of his most popular poems, titled "Frida Kahlo's Mustache," which was published after his first and only collection. But in 2015, when he received his death sentence, I was no longer translating from a publication, but rather off a verdict. I started with the fragments cited by a court of three religious judges who sought maximum punishment for the poet's words of "blasphemy" and "immorality." The more time he spent in jail, the more poems I kept on translating. Yet, I was not alone in this effort, as translators from different languages joined in. Two of those are Mona Zaki and Jonathan Wright, who gave us permission to include their translations of Ashraf's poems. Zaki translated "On the Virtues of Blood over Oil" and "The Name of a Masculine Dream" while Wright did "A Space in the Void," "The Last in the Line of Refugee Descendants," "Equal Opportunities," and "An Aphorism." We all found in translation a way to support his case, while engaging with the work and allowing it to travel into new languages.

I believe that Ashraf's poetry presents itself best. You might miss the context in few places, so I've provided footnotes that might help you navigate your reading. Many of these poems are long, sometimes as long as twenty pages. He shifts between voices, characters, and settings. He likes to break off suddenly; to leave something unfinished and start all over. Yet this very practice could make the poems enjoyable to read, as they continue to be built and destructed. He uses punctuation chaotically, brings in songs and sentences from others, and chops off lines awkwardly, piling them over each other so they become a chain of images unfolding in your hands from right to the left. So yes, this can be a challenging read -- but at the end we know that no text can be hospitable enough!

Mona Kareem

I found Ashraf's poems subtle and intriguing, indicative of a sensitive and slightly quirky interest in every aspect of the world. They're never didactic, polemical or bombastic, but often ironic, perceptive and self-deprecating. If circumstances had permitted, I would have wanted to explore the way he saw the meaning of some of his more mysterious phrases, but unfortunately this was not possible, and the reader will have to live with any misunderstandings or half-understandings I have committed.

Jonathan Wright

التعليمات بالداخل

INSTRUCTIONS WITHIN

إلى عدد هائل عرفته من الأسماء... إلى عدد ضئيل...
من حاملي هذه الأسماء

To the many names I've known...
to a few owners of those names.

حيزٌ من الفراغ

كل شيء له... وزن!
وزنك مألوف جداً للجدران الخلفية
فظلُّك الثقيل... لا يدعُ فرصةً للإسفلت
ولا للدّهانات... ولا للكتاباتِ الملصقةِ على الواجهات...
أن تظهر.
لك أيضاً حيزٌ...... لا بأس به
من ال «فراغْ»

A SPACE IN THE VOID
TRANS. JONATHAN WRIGHT

Everything has weight.
Your weight is well known to the back walls
because your heavy shadow doesn't give the asphalt a chance to appear --
or the paint, or the writings stuck on the windows.
You also have space, significant space,
in the void.

الهواء مُلوَّث... وحاويات القُمامة كذلك
وروحك منذ أن إمتَزَجَتْ بالكربون
وقلبك... منذ إغلاقِ الأوردة
ورفْضِهِ منْحَ الجنسية
للدم العائد من رأسِّك.

The air is polluted, and the dumpsters,
and your soul, too, ever since it got mixed up with carbon.
And your heart, ever since the arteries got blocked
denying citizenship
to the blood coming back from your head.

بلا ذاكرتك... تفقدُ الكثير من وزنك
عليك اتباع حميةٍ مناسبة
لفقدان المزيد منك!

Without your memory, you'd lose much of your weight.
You need to follow a proper diet
to lose more of you.

اتخذْ قرارك بسرعةٍ

فالجاذبيّةُ الأرضيةُ...

لا تنتظر كثيراً

تلميح: استبدلْ عاملَ الزمن باسمك...

حتى تصلَّ إلى الحلِّ الصحيح لكيفية إلقاء الورقةِ

الأخيرةِ من دفتر يومياتك

في سَلّة المهملات... تماماً!

Make up your mind quickly,
because the earth's gravity
doesn't wait long.
Hint: replace the factor of time in the equation with your name
so that you find the right way to throw the last page
of your diary
right into the garbage.

تستهلك من الهواء ما يكفي لمولودين جديدين...
إذا ما كان الصّراخ متساوياً...
مع العلم بأن جزيئات الهواء حولك...
تنقلُ الصوت بشكلٍ رديءٍ... وحنجرتُك...
تحتاجُ إلى الترميم.

You consume enough air for two new-born babies
if the screaming was equal,
given that the air molecules around you
carry sound badly, and your throat's
need for an overhaul.

متسوّلة تجاوزت الخمسين...تعرض وقارها في خِرْقةٍ مرصّعةٍ بالقطعِ النقديةِ... تدعو لك... ولتلك الحسناء التي تمشي بجانبك مصادفةً... بأن ترزق طفلاً قريباً حتى يشغل حيّزاً آخرَّ... من الفراغ...

مقابلَ قطعةٍ نقدية!

A beggar woman of more than fifty displays her dignity in
a rag studded with coins. In return for a coin, she prays that you (and that
pretty woman who happens to be walking beside you)
will soon be blessed with a child,
to fill another part of the void.

آن الأوان لأن تتكاثرّ خطواتك... لا جنسياً
ولأن تستبدلّ جواربك النتنة

-

-

-

حقيقة علمية: البكتيريا... تنمو بسرعة.

The time has come for you to pick up the pace --not sexually --
and for you to change your smelly socks.
.

.

.

A scientific fact: bacteria.... grow rapidly.

استسلمُ للنوم...
فقد حان الوقتُ لتسيلَ... وتتحلّلَ
ولتتخذَ الشكل المتفق عليه للغربة التي انسَكَبتّ فيها!
تبخَّر... وتكَثَّف...
وعد لفراغك...
كي تشغل حيزك المعتادّ
مِن...... الـ أنت!

Surrender to sleep.
The time has come for you to melt, and dissolve,
to take the agreed shape of alienation
into which you've been poured.
Evaporate, condense,
and go back to your void,
to occupy your usual space
of the You.

قلب

القلب مُحَرِّكٌ متقنُ الصنع...
يحتاج إلى الاحتراق... لكي يضمنَ الأداءَ المطلق!

HEART

The heart is a professionally made engine
in need of burnout to ensure maximum performance!

من فضل النفط على الدم

اعلم عافاك الله
بأن النفطَ قد انتشر وذاعّ استعمالُهُ
والنفط... كما قيل بأنَّ فيه منافع للناس.

ON THE VIRTUES OF OIL OVER BLOOD
TRANS. MONA ZAKI

Be aware, may god heal you,
that oil is spread and is loud,
and that oil, as said,
is of great benefit.

يا أيها الذين تشرّدوا...
قد شاع تشرّدكم بين الأمصار
وأفلستم
وانقطعت سُبّل خلاصِ الروح
من العدم المتفشي في أضلعكم

Oh you who have been made homeless—
your homelessness sprawled across lands,
penniless
and in despair
as oblivion unfurls between your ribs:

دمُك الأبكمُ لن ينطقُ
ما دمت تباهي بالموت
وتعلن سراً أنك قد أودعت الرّوحُ لدى من لا يفقهها.
فقدان الروح سيستغرقُ وقتاً لا يكفي
لمواساة الفزع لعينيك على ما ذرفت من نفطٍ.

Your mute blood will never speak out
as long as you brag about death,
and secretly proclaim how you've laid the soul down to those
who cannot understand it.
It will take ages to lose your soul
and console your eyes' fear for all the oil it once gushed.

وكذلك حَدَّث سيدُ قوم:
من كان له نفطٌ يقضي بالمشتقَاتِ المسفوكة منه
حوائِجُهُ...
خيرٌ ممن يوقدُ عينيه...
لكي يتّخذ من القلب إلهاً

This was what a master once said:
Whosoever has oil can meet his needs from its by-products
which is far better than he who torches his eyes—
turning the heart into a god.

لا تِمّلْكُ ما يكفي...
ليواسيك أمامَ نوائبِ هذا الدهر
لا تِمّلكُ صنبور دماء...
تُنفقه في كلّ وجوه القيم المأفوكةِ
أو ما يلزم كي تُخرج بِضعاً
من عُشر الروحِ وقد حال عليها الدهر
أو حتى ما يكفيك ليومك من غُربة.

You don't own enough
to console you in the face of time's tribulations:
you don't own a tap of blood—
to spend in the face of broken pillars,
nor do you have enough to extract
a tax on that soul of yours that time has wearied.
You don't even have enough to help you through a day of exile.

ترتعشُ الآن...
فخذ ما يتسنى من دمك
لكي تملأ بطنّ الغربةِ...
كي تحقنّ نفط المنتصبين
على نية ردتهم عن روحك.
كي تستغفر ماء النهرِ...
وتعتذر جهاراً عن دمك المتسرّب في جوفه.

You tremble now,
so take what there is of your blood
to fill the belly of exile—
to gather the overseers' oil
and smother their intention to drag away your soul.
Ask forgiveness of the river—
and loudly apologize as your blood seeps into its waters.

بالنفطِ... تقاوم!
وتفتح ما استغلق من حمّالاتِ الصدرِ
لكي ترتشف الكرزْ وما جاوره...
ولكي تنعمَّ برطوبةِ ما بين الفخذين...
وما بارَكَّت اللذةِ حوله.

It is through oil—that you resist!
As you unfasten those secured bras
and leisurely taste the cherries and all else—
and enjoy the wetness between the thighs—
may all pleasure be blessed.

ماذا بعد...

وقد علق كل المرتدّين الفأسَ على كتفك؟

وقيل بأنك من جازف بدماءٍ لا تُغني من شوق

واسترسل في تفخيخِ الخمْماراتِ بداء البهجة...

كي يشرب كأساً دون مقابل.

What next—
when all heretics have pitched the axe into your shoulder?
They say you have gambled with blood that cannot satisfy desire
and that you have filled the taverns with the malaise of joy—
in order to down a glass for free.

مجاناً

كلماتٌ مجهضةٌ

وعلبة تبغٍ مستعمل

وصندوقٌ... ألقت أمّك بصراخك فيه...

لكي يلفظك اليمُّ على ضفة خوفٍ من نوعٍ لا تألفُهُ.

حيث تعهدك الرعد بتلقيحك للغيم...

لكي تولد مطراً لا يِمسح عار الفزعِ عن النهر النائمِ

في أحضان الخيبة.

For free—
aborted words
a used tobacco pouch
and a box—where your mother once trapped your scream—
so that the river can spit you out onto the shore of fear, a kind you've never known.
And there, thunder inseminates the clouds—
rebirthing you as rain that will still be unable to wash the shame of fear from a river
sleeping in the arms of disappointment.

كريات النفط السوداء...
تتجول بين خلاياك
وتُصلِحُ ما لم يفلح غثيانَك
في تخليصك منه.

Black pellets of oil—
circulate throughout your cells
healing what your nausea
could not expel.

وما بالنفط من سوءٍ ولا ضرر

سوى ما لَوَّثَ الأجواءَ من فقرٍ يخلّفهُ

يوم تسودُ وجوه المكتشفين لبئرٍ آخر

ويُنفخُ في قلبك... كي تُبعثَ روحك نفطاً

يُستعملُ للأغراض العامة.

ذلك وعدُ النفط... إنَّ وعدَ النفط كان مفعولا.

Oil is utterly blameless
        except for its stains of poverty

on the day when the faces of those who discover another oil well turn black**
and your heart—will be filled with new life so that your soul is resurrected
as oil
for public consumption.
This is the promise of oil—a promise that will come to pass—

The end—

Almost all of this poem is quoted by the court that ruled for Ashraf's death sentence. In this line, for example, there is an allusion to Surat al Imran 3:106 of the Qur'an.

اسمُ حلمٍ مذكّر

أثناء تفانيكَ بتقديس الهمّ...
ألم تلحظ أنّ شرايينك تتخاذلُ عن ضخّ الأرق إلى
عينيك؟
ألم تلحظ؟
أن جميع قلوب المتروكين على أرصفةِ الليلِ
قد انفصلت عن عينيك مراراً؟
أنظمةُ الليل ستعمل
حين يراودها الفجرُ على أطراف الغيم المتفاقمِ
في سقفِ خيالك.
لم تلحظ أيضاً...
أنك تهوى تفسيرَ شرايين النسوةِ
والأجساد الملقاة على أسطح ذاكرةٍ فارَقَتِ الوقت
طويلاً.

THE NAME OF A MASCULINE DREAM

TRANS. MONA ZAKI

While you excel in worshipping misery—
didn't you notice that your arteries failed to pump your insomnia up to the eyes?
Didn't you notice?
That the hearts of those abandoned on the sidewalks of night
have split from your vision so many times?
The patterns of night continue their work
until dawn appears on the edges of clouds gathering
on the ceiling of your imagination.
Didn't you also notice—
how you enjoy interpreting the arteries of women
and the bodies tossed on the roofs of memories from long ago?

صفحاتُك بَلّلها التأويل
ولم يُقرأ منها غير حروف
مثلك
باتت تستنفذ كلَّ لغاتِ الأرض
لكي تصنع اسماً يُذكر في تعريفك للذات
اسمك...محبرةٌ حبلى بالتخمين
قامَتُك تنافي ما اتفق الناسُ على تعريفِ الأعضاءِ
المغروسةِ فيها

Your pages have been soaked with the sludge of exegesis
and not one word has been read
like you
these pages have exhausted all languages known to earth
in order to offer a name that matches your definition of self
your name—like an inkwell pregnant with possibilities
your build defies all definitions of its organs combined.

تعال إلى حيث يراك الرعد فيمنحك التصفية الكبرى للجسد النخِر

ويبعثُ روحك للغيم لكي يتلوها مطراً

ينهمر حياةً تعلن أن اسمك لا يرقى مرتبة الحلم

ولن يفعل ما لم تتخلَّ عن تعريف اللذات المشبوهةِ والليل الثمل

وبعض الأفواه الهاتفة بأسماء الحبِّ الحسنى.

تعال فإن الليل طويلٌ جداً للعاشق

كي يستغرق ما لا يكفي من وقتٍ ليدون لذته في أجسادٍ أمعنت في الغرق برائحةِ الدرّاق

ومارست الأقصى من كل الشهواتِ المحظورةِ في الليل.

تعال... إلى ما شاء الغيم بأن يحمل قامتك الموبوءة كي يُبعدَ روحك عن منفاها...

عن قلب صرّح رسمياً بخلو غرفه من كل بقايا الحب

وسرابات الوطن المزعومِ بأنك كنت لتنتمي إلى حَبّات ترابه.

Come stand where the thunder can see you so that your emaciated body can dissolve
and your soul be resurrected as a cloud followed by rain
pouring down life until your name is not even a dream
that won't come to pass, as long as you're unable to abandon the definitions
of dubious pleasures and drunken nights
and those who call out the sacred names of love.
Come—for the night is long for the beloved,
not long enough to write about pleasure
or bodies saturated in the smell of peaches
absorbed in all the forbidden pleasures of the night.
Come—to where the cloud chooses to shift your sickly form—
and snatch your soul from its exile
from a heart that openly declared the absence of love
and from the mirages of the assumed homeland to whose every grit of eart
you thought you belonged.

منذ متى كانت تحترم الريحُ قواعدك المرورية؟
منذ متى؟
كانت تقف الريح أمام إشارتك الحمراءِ؟
منذ متى كانت تُهادن تلك الريح
لكي تجني حفنة كلماتٍ حمَلَتها
أو أخباراً ما عادت صالحةً للنشر؟

Since when does the wind honor traffic laws?
Since when?
Did the wind ever stop at your red light?
How long have you coaxed it to stop
so you could gather a few words
or find some news that's fit to print no longer?

عيناك ستعترفان بأن الأرق
قد انتهك الحُرْمات المحفوظةَ للّيل
والليل كذلك لن يلتزم الصمتَ طويلاً.
قلبك وثن صبئت كل شرايينك عنه
وما عادت لتقدم بين يديه قرابينَ الأوردة
لكي يتقرب من عرشِ الآلهة الحسناء

Your eyes will confess that insomnia
has violated the secrets of the night
and night, too, won't keep silent for long.
Your heart is an idol to which your arteries have absconded
And they no longer offer your veins as sacrifice
as tribute to the throne of beautiful gods

اسمك لا يعنيني
لا يغفرُ لي كل خطايا القحط
ولا يشفعُ لي عند الليل لكي أخرج من عزلته
اسمك رقمٌ مفقود...
وِزْرٌ انقض ظهرك!

Your name means nothing to me
it cannot deliver me of all the sins of drought
and it cannot supplicate the night so that I can walk free from its isolation
your name is a lost number—
a weight that has broken your back!

بقعة في مجرى النهر

على ضفافِ النهر الوسخ
يتحلّق بعض الصبية
"غَرِقَتْ للتو... لعبةُ الموت..."
دجلة يبتلع الموت
ويمضي نحو الخليجِ المنكودْ

A HOARSENESS IN THE RIVER FLOW

On the banks of a dirty river
some boys make a circle
"I drowned just now.... this is a game of death...."
The Tigris is swallowing death
making its way to the doomed Gulf

"خذ العيش واغنم"
أسْمعُ صوت البحّةِ في الأذنِ اليسرى
وكذلك في أوردتي
وكذلك في النهر... وفي الغيم...وفي قلبي

***

الحلوة لم تُشرِق اليوم
الخبزُ كذلك
لا بأس فلم تعد الغربانُ تبيض على سقفي.
ضحكتُك البيضاء...
لليومِ الأسودْ!

"Embrace life to win"[**]
I hear a hoarseness in my left ear ,
in my veins
and in the river, cloud,
in my heart too

***

The sweet girl did not rise today
neither did bread
it's okay
the crows stopped laying their eggs on my ceiling.
So keep your white smile.... for a black day!

[**] *A reference to a song by the Iraqi Maqam artist Mohammed Al-Qubanchi (1900-1989).*

لا حاجة للإفطار ... فليس هنالك خبزٌ يكفي

لا حاجة للنفطٍ...

ولا للشّاي...

.

.

.

ولا لرجالِ الشرطة...

There is no need for breakfast
because there isn't enough bread;
there's no need for oil
or tea...
  .

  .

  .

nor for policemen....

النهر الوسخ يعود لكي يُنشد
لكن البحّة في صوتي لا تسمح.
أغنية تافهة...
صوت النهر المبحوح يستنزفُ صبري!
"للنهر ... بغداد تحميه"
وللقلبِ النسيان!

The dirty river returns to sing
but the hoarseness in my voice won't let it
have this stale old song.
The river's cracking voice eats away my patience!
"the river has a Baghdad to protect it"
and the heart has forgetfulness!

صرّحَ مسؤولٌ:
"ما صفالك... خذ من العيش واغنم ما بقالك...
ليالي الدهر مو كلهن سوية"
ملحوظة:
هذا مسؤول من قُوّاتِ القلب!

***

النهر اتسخ كثيراً
وهنالك بعض التعليقاتِ من الأخبار
تحليل يتبع تحليلاً.
- ماذا عن آخر أخبار الموضة؟
- ما رأيك في مجموعةِ بغداد؟

One official stated:
"take hold of what's left of life
for the nights of time are not equal"**
Note:
this is an official of the heart's militias

**

The river has gotten so dirty
comments floating on the news;
one analysis after another.
- what about fashion news?
- what do you think of the Baghdad collective?

1

** *A reference to the same song (by Mohammed Al-Qubanchi).*

هندسةٌ متقنةٌ
في تكوينِ الدومينو
عبد الجبار عنيد لا يُغلب
قصْفٌ من مهزومٍ آخر
سقط بناء الدومينو
يتراوح عدد ضحايا القصف بين فنجانين ونارجيلة

It is neatly engineered
this domino creation
Abduljabbar is stubborn and undefeated
airstrikes come from another loser
the dominos collapse
and the victims are counted between two teacups and a hookah

اغسل لذَّتك بماء النهر البارد

واعبرْ نحو المشبوقة فالظلمة حالكةٌ

خُلِقَ الليل لباساً ... لكن النهر تعرّى!

Wash out your desire with the river's cold water
then cross towards your lustful lover
as the darkness intensifies.
Although the night was made for clothing,
the river went naked!

كيف ستشرب شايك؟؟

فماء النهر قد ابتلع الموت

وأخذ يلوكُ الخيبةَ في رحلته.

نحو البصرة

تسري الخيبة

كي تتخذ مقاماً في حلقي

***

بين هجاء الحَجّاج

وتعليقات بانيبال

لا تُغمضْ عينيك

فعورة ماء السماء

قد باتت مألوفة

How can you drink your tea?
Death was eaten by the river,
chewing on defeat in his journey
towards Basra

Defeat is spreading out
settling in my throat

**

Between the satire of Hajaj
and the novelties of Banipal,
don't close your eyes
the shame of heavenly water was unveiled
and made familiar once again

أخبرْ أمك
ألا تغسلَ ثوبك
فماء النهر قد اتسخ
وعُسْر الموت قد استعمره
استفهامٌ آخر:
هل يصلحْ هذا الماء لريّ الأزهارْ؟

Tell your mother
not to wash your dress;
the river is dirty
colonized by the wretchedness of death.
Another question:
can we use the river to water flowers?

قيل: اهبطوا إليها

بعضكم للكل عدوٌّ

اهبطوا الآن منها

وانظروا من قاعِ النهر إلى أنفسكم فوق

وليمنح أعلاكم بعضَ الشفقةِ للأدنى

فَمَثَلُ المعدمين في تشرّدهم...

كدماءٍ لم تلق رواجاً في أسواقِ النفط!

You were told: settle there....
but some of you are enemies to all**
so leave it now
Then look up to yourselves from the bottom of the river;
those of you on top should have some pity on those beneath....
the displaced are helpless,
like blood in the oil market no one wants to buy!

1

**   *This line in allusion to Surat al-A'raf (7:24) of the Qur'an was also cited by the Saudi court. Edgar Allen Poe's longest poem, "Al Aaraaf" was titled after and inspired by the same Qur'anic Surah which speaks of a place between paradise and hell.*

أنا النهر المعبود
أنا الوثن الأحقر
وأنتم أصنامٌ لا أشكال لها
ونزاعات حول النهد وما جاوره
حول الكأس الرديئة ... والتبغ المتعفّنِ
وتقاريرِ الصحفيين.
وكراسي التصويت المبتذل بليل البصرة.

I am the worshipped river
I am the most worthless idol
and you are shapeless statues
arguing over breasts,
over a bad drink and rotten tobacco
and press reports
on the same old voting chairs in the Basra night.

عبد الجبّار على وشك العودة إلى المنزل
والنادل فليتكفّل بإعادة إعمارِ الدومينو...
وتسليك مسامعنا من بحة مجرى النهر...
ومن نشراتِ الأخبار.

Abduljabbar is about to return home
and the waiter will take care of resetting the dominos
and of filtering from our ears
that hoarseness in the river's flow,
and the news broadcasts.

عاشق ماجور

تحت أنقاضِ الأيام المغموسة بالقسوة
أشعُرُ بدوارٍ ... من فرط الهذيان المتحلّقِ حولي
صَخَبٌ يجتاح الليل ويسبي أحلامي
هل تصلح أن تسبى أحلامك...
أكثر من كل شريفاتِ العربِ القدماء
ومَنْ حَسُنَ النسب بهن؟
أتنكر في زي العشاق وقد زال العشق
وأعاشر ساعات الليل جميعاً.
عاشق تاريخٍ لم يُكْتَب...
صعلوكٌ أسقطه التاريخ
من الأمتعة المسلوبة في حوزة قطّاع طريقٍ لم
يتلاش
أبحثُ عن وطن أعشقه... أو يعشقني
عن بيت يؤوي كل سبايا حربٍ لم تحمل أوزاراً
كي تضع الباقي منها.
عن سقفٍ غيرِ سماءٍ
ملَّتْ من أن تَسْتُر عوْرَةِ تاريخي.

A HIRED LOVER

Under the ruins
of the days dipped-in-cruelty
I feel my head spinning....
in this inescapable delirium flying around me,
an uproar invades the night, captivating my dreams.
are your dreams more captivating
than the honorable women of ancient Arabia?
I dress up in the costume of lovers
after the decay of love
having sex until all hours of night.

A lover of a history unwritten
a tramp dropped from history,
from stolen luggage
and the outlaws who never disappear.

I am looking for a land to love.... or to love me
for a home to shelter all the captives
of a war that didn't carry any burdens
to lay them down.
I am looking for a ceiling other than a sky,
sick of veiling my shameful history

منذ نعومة أفكاري...
وأنا أتمرّس أن أعشق
كل الأوتار المشدودة فوق كمنجات الشحّاذين...
على أرصفة الوقت.
أتسلّل خلف الرغباتِ المحظورة
عمّن لم يحسن نَصْبَ شِراكِ الوهم أمام فريسته.
أحببتُ كثيراً في الماضي
لم أتردد في نطق الكلمات الأكثر إبهاراً
في كل قواميس الحب
لم أتوقّف يوماً عن تعليب القلب...
وحفظ الأشعار مبرّدةً كي تبقى جاهزةٌ للنظم...
إذا احتَجتُ إليها!

I've trained myself
to love these tight strings
on the violins of street beggars
at the sidewalks of time that matters.

I sneak behind the prohibited desires
of someone less artful
in creating illusions for his prey.

I fell in love many times
in the past
I did not hesitate
to say the most impressive words
in the dictionaries of love
I never stopped packaging my heart
and keeping the poems refrigerated
ready for writing
in case I needed them!

هذي حسناء... وتلك كما الماء الجاري
تلك هنالك وطنٌ... يا للوطن المتحضّر!
أتقَنْتُ حواراتِ النهدين
ومناظرة الأجساد جميعاً
وخرجتُ من الوطن وعدت إليه مراراً
لكن الوطن المجهد ما عاد ليتسع الآن
إلى قلبٍ أضحى كالفندق.
قدّمتُ الخدماتِ الفاخرةَ جميعاً
وحرصتُ على أن تتمتع كل نزيلاتي بالراحة...
بالدفء ...وبالأمن المتناهي
ونسيت بأن الفندق لم يوجد يوماً للسكنِ الدائم.
ونسيت بأن الفندق أيضاً...
يحتاج إلى أرضٍ... وطنٍ يُبنى فيه!

That one is pretty... and that one is like running water
but that one is a homeland.... oh, what a civilized one!
I excelled in the dialogues of bosoms
and the debates of bodies

And I left the homeland
returning again and again
but this exhausted home is too packed now
for a heart-turned-hotel.

I offered fancy services
and made sure all my guests felt comfortable
warm
and infinitely safe... .
but I forgot that a hotel
was never meant to be a lasting home
and I forgot
that a hotel needs land too;
a homeland to be built on!

في الحي الخلفي... يُقيم العاشق
ينظُم أشعاراً... يرسُم لوحاتٍ
يبني ألواناً باهتةً
كي يعرضها في أروقة متاحفِ ذكرى الليل.
هذا الحي البائس يستقطبُ آفات الأرق الدائم...
والأشباح الخائفة... وقلوب نساءٍ مكسورة
يؤوي الأقمار الخائفة...
ويهدي المدن المكتظة عشاقاً.
انتَخَبَ الحيُّ العشاق... فكنت الأكثر أرقاً
أهداني الأرقُ إلى المدن المتعبة...
فقَطعتُ الآفاق وأمعنَ قلبي في العشق
وأوقدَ كلَّ الرغباتِ الغارقةَ بماء النسيان
أتقنتُ فنون الحب... ومارستُ الأقسى منها
داعبتُ نهودَ الوهم... وروّضتُ النافر منها
واصلتُ طريقي حتى لامستُ الأفق الناعم
واتكأت روحي فوق وسادته...

**

In the back neighborhood, the lover resides
writing poems, drawing paintings,
making up tasteless colors
to showcase in the museum corridors of night memories.
This sad neighborhood attracts
the diseases of permanent insomnia,
the scared ghosts.... and the hearts of broken women.
Sheltering scared moons
guiding cities packed with lovers.
The neighborhood elected his lovers....
and of them I slept the least.
Insomnia had led me to exhausted cities
cutting horizons and sinking in love,
flaming my desires
after soaking me in the water of forgetfulness.
I mastered all arts of love and practiced the cruelest of them
I played with the bosoms of illusion
and tamed the most reluctant of them
I kept walking until I touched the sleeping horizon
laying my soul down on its pillow.

حتى استيقظ وهمُ الرؤية في أخيلتي.
كانت تجربة زاهرة باللامعنى!
كل المدن الآن تحدّقُ في خطواتي...
أين ستحملني الآن؟!
أين ستُبعد شبحاً كان مثيراً للهلع
لدى سكان الأحياءِ المكتظّةِ بالنسوة؟
كابوساً كنتُ وكانت خطواتي تحملني
نحو المبهم من طرقِ العزلةِ
عن مجتمعات الشرف الأبدي.
خانتني حتى خطواتي
حمَلَتني نحو المنفى الفردي بعيداً....
عن وطنٍ لم أعرف أرصفةً لموانئه.
علِقَت في أنفي رائحةُ الوطن
وكانت ذاكرتي تحمل قطعاً من لحظات
لم أنسها...

Until the illusion of a vision vanished from my imagination,
it was an experience full of nonsense.
All cities now are staring at my steps...
where are you taking me?
where are you taking the ghost who frightened
most of that neighborhood packed with women?
I was a nightmare
my steps carrying me towards the unknown
towards lonely roads
away from the societies of eternal honor.
I was betrayed even by my steps
they took me far into exile…
away from a homeland
that had no ports.
The smell of home is stuck in my nose
and in my memory there remain fragments never to be forgotten.

كانت تلك القطع تسكّن آلام الغربة
كانت تبعث في قلبي...
غليانَ الشوقِ الهادر في الدم المجبر أن يتدفق في أوردتي.
تأتيني نوباتُ الشوق مراراً
تلتهم فتات الصبر المنثور على مائدتي.
وتؤجّجُ كل الرغبات الجامحة بأن أرجع يوماً.
لكن الوطن بعيد... جداً
وليس لديّ وسيلةُ نقل ترجعني.
ما عاد القلب ليقوى أن يحملني....
أو حتى يحمل شوقاً وحنيناً
أو عشقاً... أو أن تنزل فيه مسافرة أخرى...
تبحث عن دفءٍ يُشبعُ رغبتها.

They calmed my pains of exile
but flamed my heart with a longing
that coursed through the veins.
The seizures of yearning overtake me often
eating the crumbs of patience left on my table.
They stir my wild desires to return one day.
but home is far…away
and I have no means of transportation.
This heart cannot carry me anymore
nor my longing and nostalgia and love;
nor can it host another traveller
seeking to satisy that insatiable desire for warmth.

**

أمضيتُ طويلاً وأنا أشبعُ كل الرغبات
أمنح أصناف الدفء لمن يبحث عنها
وأثير قضايا الحي البائس كي أجعل من هذا البؤس مثالاً
كي أصنعَ من كمنجاتِ الشحاذين...
نشيداً وطنياً للعشاق
لأزيل الحظرَ عن الحب المأسور لدى أطفالِ الوحشة.

For too long,
I was fulfilling all desires
giving all sorts of warmth for those seeking it
bringing up the matters of the sad neighborhood
to make its sadness exemplary,
to author a national anthem for lovers
out of homeless violins,
and lift the ban on a love
captivated by the children of desolation

في أحد الأحلام...
أتيتُ من المنفى
كي أُعلنَ أني أقلعتُ عن الحب.
أحببت مراراً...
كي أبني أرصدةً ملء خزائنها
أجساد إناثٍ يؤويها القلب...
ويحفظها الشبقُ من النسيان المتفشّي في مُدنِ المنفى.
كي أرجع يوماً وأنا أحمل أوسمةً...
تخفي القلب المتعب عن مرمى أبصارِ الوطن المتلهف للعودة منتصراً.
أبليت بلاءً حسناً...
وأنا ألتقطُ الأجساد وأهمل عمداً
ما حَمَلْتُهُ قلوب النسوة من جناتٍ
تكتظ بداخلها أنهارٌ تؤوي كل المدن المنفية...
عن كتب التاريخ.

In one of the dreams
I returned from exile
to announce that I had quit love.
I fell in love many times
filling my accounts
with female bodies
sheltered in my heart
preserved by desire
against the forgetfulness common
to exile cities.
To return one day
carrying medals
is to hide a heart
exhausted by the distance
from a home hungry for victory.
I did well....
picking up bodies
and neglecting the women
who had carried heavens in their hearts;
where rivers and exiled cities
stay out of history's sight.

**

أرجعُ... لكنّي أرجع في أحد الأحلام
في إحدى المحظورات الألف...
لدى مدن المنفى.
أرجعُ...
في إحدى نوباتِ الشوقِ الجامحة...
لدى قلب العاشق...
في المنفى.

I return... but I return in a dream,
in one of the thousand prohibitions
of exile cities.
I return
following a seizure of wild longing
that had attacked the heart
of an exiled lover.

بنتٌ وولد...
الأم تفضّل الولد على البنت.
الولد سيقف بجوار أمه عند نوائبِ الدهر
البنت ستنجب ولداً آخر ليقفَ بجوارها!

EQUAL OPPORTUNITIES

TRANS. JONATHAN WRIGHT

A son and a daughter.
The mother prefers the son to the daughter.
The son will stand by his mother through the ups and downs of life.
The daughter will make another son to stand by her side.

قوانين الوطن الثلاثة

القانون الأول:

كل وطنٍ آمن... أو في حربٍ مستمرة...
كل وطنٍ تطأه قدماك كل يوم... ولا يتذمر...
يظل في القلب... ما لم تؤثر عليه غربة من الذات...
تُفقِدْهُ الأهمية.

THE THREE RULES OF HOME

First Rule:

Every home is safe.... or in an ongoing war,
every home you step into without complaint
will remain in your heart....
Unless he is made upset by an alienation of the self
that strips him of value.

القانون الثاني:

الغربة المؤثرة في روحٍ لا كتلة لها...
تتناسب طردياً مع هذيانك...
مع وهم الاستقرار...
مع كل أكاذيبِ الطقس...
ومع أصوات السياراتِ المزدحمة...
ومع نسبة النيكوتين في دمك.

Second Rule:

the alienation of a shapeless soul
is in direct proportion with your rants—
and with the illusion of stability,
lies about the weather,
the traffic noise,
and the percentage of nicotine in your blood.

القانون الثالث:

لكل فقدان...
وجودٌ مفترض...
ولكل فراغ... ملء فراغ
ولكل حي مزدحم... فناء
يَقِلُّ عنه في الحجم
ويعاكسه في الازدحام
فالجيران ينامون طوال الوقت
لأنك وحدك!

Third Rule:

Every loss
has a presumed existence...
every void
can be filled with void
and every packed neighborhood
has a courtyard;
smaller in size
yet countering the traffic.

the neighbors sleep all the time
because you are alone!

أذكارٌ للشوق

بغصنٍ من الشوك...
أُسرّحُ شعري... أجمعُ خصلاته...
علك تجمعني بين ذراعيك.

***

قالوا أن هناك حصاراً قد ألغي
وبأن يديك المستهلكتين...
قد أُوقِفَ عن ضمهما القيد.
وبأني قد ألقاك... كما قالوا

PRAYERS OF LONGING

with a leaf of thorns
I comb my hair... gathering the curls,
the way you would gather me in your arms.

***

they said a siege was canceled
and that your worn-out hands
are no longer embraced with shackles.
and that I might meet you

مَرَّت... لا أعرف كم...

مَرَّت؟

لا أعرف

كم... مَرَّت؟

كم عجفاء...وكم من خيطٍ فضّي طَرَّزَهُ الزَّمن

على رأسي.

I don't know how much time passed...
passed?
I don't know
how much... passed?

how much waste...
and how many silver threads in my head
time had woven

اغفِر لي تكرار وفاتكَ فوق سريري
اغفِر لي نسياني رائحة العرق المنهك فوق فراشك
لا حبيب إلا أنت... إني كنت من القانطين

pardon me, for your repeated death on my bed
forgive me for forgetting the smell of exhausted sweat
on your bed

There is no lover but you; for I have been in despair

عفوك... اغفِر لي
إضرابي عن ضخّ الدمع
عن تكرار اسمك آناء الشوق
وأطراف الوحشة.
إني وجّهتُ وجهي بحثاً عن دفء ذراعيك
لا حبيب إلا أنت... وحدك... وأنا أول العاشقين

pardon me, forgive me;
for not being able to pump more tears for you
for not mumbling your name in longing and loneliness.
I direct my face towards the warmth of your arms
I've got no lover but you, you alone,
and I'm the first of your seekers.

عناوين

(الحَجَّاجُ) يُقَلِّد (روبي) وسام بابل البلاستيكي
في حفل ضخم...
إعلانٌ في الإنترنت عن الحاجة إلى متطوعين
في حرب (البسوس)...
ومحاولاتٌ جادة للوصول إلى (قارون) في أعماق
الأرض ليجيب عن استفساراتِ المستثمرين عبر
هاتفٍ مجاني!

TITLES

In a grand celebration,
al-Hajjaj presents Rubi** with the plastic medal of Babylon...
An ad on the internet is seeking volunteers
for the Basus war...
While the serious attempts to reach "Korah" continue
to dig the depths of earth
so he can answer the questions of investors
in a free consultation call!

** *Egyptian pop singer.*

ليل شاعر

تحت الفزع المتساقط في ليلي
تقبعُ كلُّ الاسئلةِ المشبوهة
تعلن أن الليل سيمضي... دون إجابة
لا فرق... فكل الليل كذلك
كل الليل يناور شهوات الرعد
وبهجة كل الغيمات المكسوة بالوحدة

VACANT NIGHT

Under the falling horror of my night
all suspicious questions reside
declaring that the night will go on.... unanswered.
No difference.... for all night is one
maneuvering desires of thunder
and joy of clouds, clothed in loneliness.

يَستغربُ كل رعاة النجم أني أبتذل الوقت

وألقي خلف خطاي

القادمَ من سكَرات الليل.

كانت دور اللهو تراقبُ همّي

وتحاول تجنب صفعات كادت تعتاد أن تخطئ وجهي...

ذلك قدري

قدري أن أتقاطعَ مع كل النزوات المشبوهة

بين الغيم وبين الرعد

وبين الأجرامِ المنفية...

مدَّعياً أني أتقن الهطول على حَبّات الرمل

لكي أصنع منها نُصباً للإنسان.

the star shepherds find it strange
that I exploit time
throwing future intoxications
behind my steps.
The clubs went on watching my worries
trying to avoid the slaps which no longer miss
the way to my face....
That is my destiny,
my destiny—to intersect
with all these suspicious fantasies
between cloud, thunder,
and astronomical objects in exile....
I claim to have mastered
the act of raining on sand grains
in order to make a memorial for mankind.

وأحاول أن أتذكر

أين طريقي نحو الرمل؟

وأين يكون الإنسان على هامشِ جسد الليل؟

فرقٌ... أن تبحث في جسد الليل

وأن تبحث في جسدك عن شوقك إلى الليل

وشوقك أيضاً لزيارة تلك المعجونة باللوز

لكي تتلو المتيسر من جسدٍ أربكه إمعانُ الليل

بمزج رحيق الفاكهة المجبولة باللذة.

أن تبحث عن عينين لكي تلقي

بالجسد المتهالك في خدرهما.

I try to remember
where the way is to the sand
and where man is on the bodily margin of night?
There is a difference... to look for the body of night
and to search your body for a longing for night.

There's a difference
in longing to visit a woman of almond
and recite to her from a body
made nervous by the depth of night.
There's a difference
if you ever find the eyes
that could host your decaying body in their restfulness.

عارٌ أن تتلو الجسد

وأن تخرج عن دستورٍ

ما أنزل فيه الليل أو الجسد المتهالكُ من سلطان

فلابد من القلب لكي تعشق

والقلب....

يقال بأن القلب سيولد حين يعودُ الإنسان

It is a shame to recite the body
and to go against a constitution
of sacred words
for you need the heart
to love
and the heart
will only be born when humans return

أثقلَك المطر بصفحات الإعلان الباهظة
لكي تبحث عن حبات الرمل...
عن الطينِ المتقاعدِ
عن فزع الليل إذا أدركه جُرْمٌ...
يخترق غلاف عيون لم تعرف طعمَ النومِ طويلاً.

the rain overloaded you with
pages of expensive ads
so you searched for grains of sand,
the retired mud,
and the horror of night
when hit with an object
cutting through eyes
unfamiliar with the taste of sleep.

عارٌ...
أن تبحث عن قلب
والمطر اختارَك أن تحيا قلباً...
يتسع لشتى أعراق الإنسان المتفشي فيك...
وفي لوحات الإعلان المحجوزة لليل.
ليلُ شاغرٌ......
يحتاج إلى عاشق.
يحتاج إلى من يُتقنُ لغةَ المطر...
وبعض مهارات الإنسان

What a shame
to look for a heart
when the rain has chosen you to be one
wide enough for all human kinds....
On the billboards of night,
the vacant night is searching for a lover
for someone fluent in the language of rain
and other human skills.

يحتاجُ إلى أنثى...
بارك حول مباهجها ماء العشق
وعمَّدها الغيم بما يتلوه المطر...
على أسماعِ الجسد المعجونِ بعطر اللوز
وحبات الثلج العائمة على كأس رحيقٍ
يستفسر عن معنى الفجر الغارق بين النون
وتاء التأنيث وخاتمة الهاء المزهوة ثملاً

He is looking for a female
to bless her joys with the water of love
baptized by clouds
in the presence of a body
clayed with the smell of almonds
to the sounds of ice cubes floating in the glass...
He is questioning the meaning of a dawn
drowning between the N, the feminine T, and the drunk H of endings.**

** *These letters refer to the feminine suffixes in the Arabic.*

يحتاج إلى زخّاتٍ من ماء الروح
وغيم كي يصطنع المطر
وبعضٍ من كلماتِ الشوق
وشهاداتٍ يعترف بها المنفى
ليمارسَ كل طقوس العشق الخارقة لأنظمة الليل.

This body needs showers of soul water,
clouds to make rain with,
words of longing,
and degrees recognized in exile
to practice all the love rituals
that could overthrow the regime of Night.

ليلٌ...
تنقُصُه الخبرة بالوقت
وتنقصُهُ زخات المطر
لتغسلَ كل عوالق ماضيك الضالة
وتمنحَك خلاصاً مما كنت تسميه العفة
والقلب القادر بهتاناً أن يعشق...
أن يلهو؛
أن يتقاطع مع ردتك السافرة عن الدين الرخو
عن التنزيلِ الزائفِ
عن تصديقك بآلهة ضَلَّت عزتها.

Night,
you are inexperienced with time
lacking raindrops
that could wash away the remains of the past
and free you of chastity
and of a heart that can love and play
asserting your abandonment
of a flaccid religion, a fraud revelation,
and of faith in gods
who had lost their pride.

حكمة

الحب ليس أن تكون عصفوراً في يدِ من تحب...
خيرٌ له من عشرة على الشجرة
عصفورٌ على الشجرة خيرٌ من عشرةٍ في اليد...
من وجهة نظر العصافير!

AN APHORISM
TRANS. JONATHAN WRIGHT

To be in love is not to be a bird in the hand of the one you love,
better for them than ten in the bush.
A bird in the bush is better than ten in the hand,
from the birds' point of view.

مَتلازمة الوطن ... الحادّة

أعراض أولية:

ترتفع حرارة تصفيقِ المتفقين على توديعك.
إرهاقٌ... يسبق تجهيزاتك للسفر على راحلةٍ تبدو
مثلك
موسومٌ أولها بنحيبٍ يسبقُك حيث تولّي وجهك.
متبوعٌ أنت بكل اللعناتِ المألوفة عند أساطيرِ القدماء.

THE SEVERE SYNDROME OF HOME

Early symptoms:

the increasing heat of those clapping at your departure.
the exhaustion.... before you travel on this vehicle resembling you,
marked with a wailing that will be awaiting you at your destination,
followed by all the spells known in ancient myths.

نتائج الفحص:

في هذا... الـ حين
تعاني ما يشبه نشوة مذهولٍ بعارضةٍ تتعرّى!
وتبدع في كيل شتائمك لماضيك العفن.
وتُكثر من رقصك في صالاتِ الاستقبال...
وأروقة الفنادق...
والشوارع الرئيسية.
يكثر سيلان لعابك
ويصغر بؤبؤ عينيك.
في هذا الـ حين
تسمى مغترباً.

Results:

Meanwhile, you suffer the pleasure
of someone amazed by a stripping pole;
you get creative at cursing your damned past.
you dance much at the lobbies,
in the hotel corridors,
and on the main streets.
You drool
as your eyes shrink.
Only then, you are called a stranger.

الأعراض:

تضخُّمٌ في الهذيان...وإفراطٌ في الأرق...وهالاتٌ
سوداء حول نوافذ غرفتك وحول الأضواء المتنازِعة
في المدن...ونزيفٌ حاد في تمديدات القلب...يصحبه
غثيانٌ يُعزى للقلق الناتج من تحليل تسكعك المشبوه،
اختناق يصاحب حديثك عن نفسك...عن ليلاك...
وعن بضعة رموزٍ آمنت قديماً بها.
تدنٍّ ملحوظ في استيعابك للمارة
وترنح ساقيك خلال المشي بدون مسافات
وخلال جلوسك أيضاً
ونشاطٌ لانمطي في إحصاء الخطوات المستهلكة
على كل الأرصفة

Symptoms:

An inflammation of delirium, excess insomnia, black halos
circulate the windows of your room and the disputed lights of the cities.
Extreme bleeding in the heart pipes, accompanied by nausea
caused by the anxiety of your suspicious loitering…
you suffocate as you speak about yourself…. about your night….
and about some idols you used to believe in.
You clearly fail to notice the passersby
and your swinging legs as they're walking no distances
or sitting
or through the unusual activity of counting
how many steps you've consumed on the sidewalks

ونقصٌ حاد

في كريات الرغبة داخل أوردتك.

تتجشأ... أكثر مما اعتدت بأن تفعل

والحانات تبارك ما تتلوه على أسماع المخمورين...

وأجساد الغانيات التي تنفُثُ فيها...

ويصحبك الـ D.J

عند تصاعد ترتيلك الهذيانَ

وتسبيحَك باسم الأجساد المتمايلة على آيات الغربة.

You suffer from an acute shortage
in the cells of desire in your veins.
You burp more than you used to,
yet the bars bless you as you recite
to the drunken visitors
and the night dancers
whose bodies you breathe in
Accompanied by the D.J
your recital ascends in hallucination
and you pray in the name of
these bodies swinging
to your verses of exile.

وتعود لتستلقي فوق آرائك لم تَندِفْ أمك فيها قطناً
وتعتنق أساليبَ لم تألفها للنوم
لكي تستخدمه في بعض الأغراضِ المتعلقة
بجدوى صحوك...
وبجدوى تنقيبك عن وجهك...
بين البِرَك الراكدة وواجهات المحالّ التجارية....
كي تدلي ببصاقك حيث يليق به أن يهطل.
وتصاب بصدأ في الروح
يتخلل بحثَك عن وجهك في قطرات المطر...
وفي عوادم السيارات...
وفي روزناماتٍ...انتهت صلاحيتها.
كي تتذكر...
وتمزق ذاكرتك
كي تتوهم أنك مخلوقٌ تَنسَى
وتشرب وحدك... نخبَ المطر
ونخب السيارات... ونخبَ الضوضاء بمجملها

Then you return
to lay down on beds
that your mother didn't comb with cotton.
You try new sleeping methods
so you can be ready
to justify your wakefulness
and to search for your face
in the still pools and the shopfronts....
You want to spit in the right place.

Hit with a rustiness in the soul,
you search for a face in the raindrops,
in car exhaust, and in expired calendars....
To remember, then
to rip out the memories
and to fantasize about being a creature of forgetfulness,
You drink alone.... to the rain
to the cars.... and to all that noise around

العلاج:

كذّب كل الأخبار... وأقوال الصحف
وتحليلات المختصين بآخر أخبار الموضة.
لا تُفرِط في النوم ولا في استخدامِ الهاتفِ
المحمول.

ومارس بعض التمرينات... على الموت.
تخلص من كل الصور التي تحملها
من طفولتك ومراهقتك وفقرك
وحبيبتك السابقة ...وحكايا جدّتك.
وتسَلُّلِ جسدك ليلاً للعبث بما يدعى أعراضاً.
استخدم الماء الساخن أثناء استحمامك
وغسيل قدميك كلما خلعتَ الجوارب
واستعن بتجارب من هم بعدك
اكتب اسما مقلوباً في المرآة
كل بيمينك...
واترك ما يليك لمن هو أجدر منك بلقمتك المغموسةِ بالنفط.

Cure:

Do not believe the news and the newspapers
and the analyses of fashion experts.
Do not exaggerate in your sleep
or while using your cellphone.
Exercise some death.
Get rid of the pictures that carry
your childhood, adolescence, poverty,
your ex, your grandmother's tales,
and your sneaking body at night messing with the so-called symptoms.
Take hot showers
and learn from those who come after you
write your name flipped on the mirror
eat with your right hand....
and leave what comes after
to someone more deserving of this
food dipped in oil than you.

الله... لنا!!!
خَلَقَنا من طين
وجَعَل لكل داءٍ دواء
وجعل لكل سليمٍ سقماً
ولكل مبتهجٍ بكاء!
تلحّف بغنائك
ولا تتعرّض للشوق مباشرة.

.

.

.

.

.

فرص الشفاء ضئيلة
اتبع التعليمات المكتوبة على ظهر المرآة
واحفظ صورتك بعيداً عن متناولِ يديك!

God is ours!
He made us out of mud
and for every illness he made a cure;
for the healthy he brought sickness
and for the joyful he made tears!
Wrap yourself with songs
and don't get directly exposed to longing.
.
.
.
.

your chances to be cured are slim
so follow the written instructions on the back of the mirror
and keep your picture away and out of reach!

حظك لهذا اليوم

عطارد يصطدم بالقمر نتيجة خلاف قديم!
صديقٌ قديم يتصل بك فجأة ليستفسر عما إذا كانت
(هيفاء وهبي) هي نفسها التي ظهرت عارية
في أحد مقاطع الفيديو المشبوهة.
وحب قديم يطفو على السطح
(لا تطفو عادة إلا الأجسام الميتة)!

YOUR LUCK TODAY

Mercury crashes into the moon due to an old dispute!
an old friend calls you out of nowhere to inquire
whether it was Haifa Wahbe herself in that porn video.
And an old love floats on the surface
(though only dead bodies usually float)!

حزنٌ من عجين

بعضك يتراكم فوق بعضٍ... ومزيج من دمك

وعَرَقك... وبقاياك... وما تفرزه عيناك

وما......... تفرزه عيناك

وعقدة لسانك... عند انتصاف البحر

وعند سباحة قرص الشمس...

في فلك مسبق التحديد

تعقيد......!

A MELANCHOLY MADE OF DOUGH

Parts of you pile one on top of another—a mixture of your blood,
sweat, remains, and the discharge from your eyes.
That discharge of your eyes and the knot of your tongue
meet the sea at a midpoint,
where the sun sphere swims
in a preconceived orbit—
What complications!

ما لم يذكُرهُ الرصيف

أنك كنت تدوسُ ... عليه

وتقدم نعليك على طبق من اسمنت

وقدميك على طبق من نعليك

وساقيك على طبق من خيبتك

وتدوزن رأسك كي تتصنع بهجتك الساذجة

وتواري جمجمة... لا ترغب أن تحملها

تتراكم فوق لوحٍ يزعم البياض بحفنة دقيق...

وتتخمر.

تنتفخ وتنفث حزنك كرغيفٍ ساخن

وتيبس.

تبحث عن مائك...

بين ليونتك وتيبّسك...

وتكسُّرك.

ويحمرُّ جبينك

أيضاً... كرغيف!

What the sidewalk never mentioned
is that you used to step on it
presenting your shoes on a plate of concrete,
your feet on a plate of shoes,
and your legs on a plate of disappointment.
You tune the strings of your head faking a naive joy,
hiding a skull you'd rather not bear.
You pile yourself on a slate that claims whiteness with a fist of flour—
until fermentation.
You are swelling, puffing your sadness like a hot loaf
until you dry.
Searching for your water,
between delicacy and hardness
and crumbling.
Your forehead reddens,
also, like a loaf!

تُحْفَظ

في الذاكرة العشوائية

للأرض... لباطنها

للوح المحفوظ... على كتفيك

....

تتعفن...أيضًا...كرغيف!

....

وتقاوم عبثاً تقلُّب جسدك فوق اللوح المبيض

فوق فراشك...

فوق الأرصفةِ... وفوق الأسطحِ العاكسة

والمنعكسة...

والممتصةِ الضوء.

ينسى جسمك دوماً...أنك مزيجٌ معقد

أنك لا تملك غير الشكل المألوف لساقيك

أنت في هيئة متشرد

تختلفُ ملامحه عمن يخطون الخطواتِ الأخرى

لا يتقن مشيتهم... لا يتحدث بلغتهم.

You get stored
in the chaotic memory
of earth, in its core,
in the "preserved tablet" on your shoulders.
…

You grow mold, also, like a loaf!
…

In vain, you resist your body's floundering on the whitened slate
of your bed...
on the sidewalks, on the reflecting
and reflected surfaces,
absorbing light.
Your body always forgets its complex mixture,
and that you got nothing but the familiar look of your legs
resembling a homeless man
whose features stand out amongst the passers-by;
He can neither master their walk nor speak their language.

لا يملك حقاً في أن يمشي كما يشاء
ويترنح كما يشاء ويبكي كما يشاء.
لا يملك حقاً في أن يفتح شباك الروح
ليجدّدَ هواءها...وهباءها... وبكاءها.
تنسى أنت...كذلك أنك...أيضاً
....كرغيف!

He's got no right to walk however
or to stumble however or to cry however.
He's got no right to open the window of his soul,
to renew his air and waste and tears...
You too tend to forget that you are
a loaf of bread!

تنسى كيف امتزجت روحك...
منذ ولدتَ... ومنذ قُطعت مشيمتك.
امتزجت...روحك...امتزجت
بملابس تخفي سوءتك...
وتكشف ما يظهر منها ... منك
ومن نسوة اعتدن... شقَّ جيوبهن
وتعليق الصور على الجدران.
من فتيةٍ...احترفوا ... الرسمَ على الجدران
وعلى شواهد القبور... وعلى سيارات الخردة
والتظاهر باسمك....أيضاً...
كرغيفْ!
وامتزجت روحك...
وتجانَسَت... وتخَمَّرت...وعُجنت...وخُبزت
وبيعت في متاجر مخالفة للشروط الصحية
وزُوِّرت... واستخدمت للأغراض اللامشروعة
وتم التصويت عليها
ثم التُهمَت...أيضاً...
كرغيفْ....!

You forget how your soul got mixed
at birth, when they ripped your placenta.

Your soul was dressed
in clothes that conceal your genitals
and reveal what may be seen of them, of you,
of the women who have grown accustomed to ripping their own collars
and hanging pictures on the walls.
Of the boys who have mastered their drawing skills
on walls and gravestones and junk cars
while marching in your name, also,
like a loaf!

So your soul is all mixed:
homogenized, fermented, kneaded, baked
and sold at stores
that violate standards of hygiene…

Your soul was forged and used for illegal purposes,
voted on—
then eaten
like a loaf.

منطق

الباب القديم يُصفّق للريح...
على استعراضها الراقص برفقة الأشجار!
الباب القديم... ليس لديه كفّان.
والأشجار لم تلتحق بمعهد تعليم الرقص.
والريح، كائنٌ غير مرئي...
حتى عندما ترقُصُ مع الاشجار.

LOGIC

The old door applauds the wind
for its dancing performance with the trees.
The old door has no hands
and the trees were not trained at a dancing school.
The wind is an invisible creature,
even when it's dancing with the trees.

ج.ا.م

يصطفّون على قارعة المرآة؛
على الصفحات المرموقة
قطعان وجوه تتسللُ كي تختم بالبصقات المجانية
أنت وأنتم....
حسناً....
أنتن كذلك... هنّ... وهم:
788-899-76777-213
وأضف ما شئت ن/م

B.I.M.

They line up on the sidewalks of the mirror
on the numbered pages
flocks of faces sneaking in
to be stamped with free spit
you and you
alright
you too and them and they:
213-76777-899-788
and add more if you want

خفافاً وثقالاً يمتصون النكهة كاملةً
مختلف الأشياء ستدعمها رائحةُ العرق المتمازج
اهبطوا...!
وهبطوا... وتناسلوا... وتعاقبوا
حبات ترابٍ... نُطفٌ... أمشاجٌ... مُضَغٌ... وعظامٌ تتكدس
ولحمٌ مختلفة أثمانه
لا يذوقون فيها... إلا النكهات المجهولة
والمستنكرة على وجوه الأعراف...
وكل تقاليد ولوج الليل
وتفسير رطوبة ما بعد المدخل
وهبطوا... وتناسلوا... وتعاقبوا
حبات تراب... أرقام متسلسلة

Light and heavy they suck out all the flavor
all different things will be backed with the smell of mixed sweat
come here...!
come here and breed and keep on
sand grains, semen drops, blood mixtures, lumps, and bones
piling up
meat at different prices
of unknown tastes
condemned by all customs
and traditions
of night-entering
and the interpretations of humidity post entrance.
Come here and breed and keep on
sand grains and serial numbers
and semen drops and other numbers!

نطف... أرقام أخرى!

مضغ... ولحم مختلفة أثمانه...

و21563478:

وكذلك:4128567

أيضاً:01000101011010101

من؟؟؟

قلنا: 01000100111

عفواً: 01000101011010101

لا فرق... سوى خاتمة الهاء

وفاتحةِ الألف المفترضة

لا فرقَ... سوى حجمِ النهدين... ولونِ العينين...

وقُطرِ الأردافِ... وطولِ الأعضاء...

وسعةِ الأرحام... ورقم أو رقمين

وكثرة ما في الجيب... وملء الأرصدة

ورائحة العطر... ونوع السيارة... وحجمِ السكن

وماركاتِ الأحذية... وعنوانِ الخياطة.

وبضعةِ أرقامٍ أخرى.

Lumps and meat of all prices
and: 21563478
as well as: 4128567
also: 01000101011010101
who????
excuse me: 01000101011010101
No difference... except for the ending H
and the opening A
No difference.... except for breast size.... and eye color
the diameter of hips and the length of organs
the width of wombs.... one or two numbers.
No difference.... except for the heavy pockets and bank accounts
the perfume smell, the car type, the house size
the shoe brands and the tailor's address.
And some other numbers.

01011001010011101110110 1

01011001010011101110110 1

01011001010011101110110 1

قارن واختر ما يقبله العالمُ منك

أنا

10001

أنا

000

أنا

1

01000101011010101
01000101011010101
01000101011010101
compare and choose what the world accepts of you
I am
10001
I am
000
I am
1

لا شيءَ من المذكور يُطابق ما أمليناه عليك
أعِدِ الكرّة
فأنتم حشراتٌ تحتاجُ إلى بعض التنظيم
وللترقيم وللـــ... حصر والتعديل
ـ كفى ثرثرةً!
واصل عملك في صمتٍ
فللعمل خصالٌ محمودة!
وللأرقام المتبقية من كل خلاياكم
عودوا للصف...
وعودوا للترقيم
عودوا... أو فليتكفل من يتطوع منكم
لإعادة تصنيف المستهلك منكم.
أنتم......... أسماء... أشياء...
تفتقر إلى التنظيم!

None of the above satisfies what we've demanded of you
try again
you are insects in need of some arrangement,
of numbering, listing, and adjustment
- cut the talk!
keep working in silence
labor is good!
and for the numbers left in your cells
return to the lines
to the numbering
go back... or some of you could volunteer
to categorize the rest of you
You are... names... things
in need of arrangement.

مساواة

قيل بأن الناسَ كأسنان المشط
لكنهم ليسوا كذلك... سأحلق رأسي على كل حال
كي لا أضطرَّ للمقارنة.

EQUALITY

It is said people are like the teeth of a comb**
but they are not... anyway, I'll shave my head
so I won't be forced into the comparison!

**   *"All people are equal, like the teeth of a comb. There is no claim of merit of an Arab over a non-Arab, only God-fearing people merit a preference with God." - attributed to the Prophet Mohammed.*

غراب... يطير على عكازين

غراب... يطير على عكازين

الريش الأسود

لا يتفق مع التقليعاتِ السائدة الآن

لا يتفق وأسلاك الكهرباء

ولا مع جُثثٍ

عُدِّلت كي لا تتعفن

A CROW FLYING ON CRUTCHES

black feather
does not go well with new trends
or with the electricity wires
or with the corpses
fixed not to rot

كان الله على العرش

يستمع الى التسبيح المضاد

ويعاقبك طوالَ الوقت...

على حومتك المشبوهة فوق الجثثِ المعطرة.

الله على العرش...

خلق الطيرَ... وعلّمه الطيران

وعلّمه أن يسعى للرّزق

ويسقط... كل السقطات المحظورة والمسموح بها.

Sitting on the throne
God was listening to your counter prayers
always punishing you
for your suspicious roaming over the perfumed corpses.
God on the throne
He created bird and taught him to fly
and to search for a living
in all permitted and prohibited slips.

الله على العرش

وأنت الآن تحاولُ إصلاحَ جناحيك

وأنت هنا

تتعلّمُ درساً

مما فاتك

مما يفعله الطيرُ

ومما يستصلح من ريش أجدب

لم يمسسه الماءُ طويلاً.

الله... على العرش

يسلب منك الطيران لكي لا تختلس النظر

إلى أسطح مدنٍ لا تألف حومتك...

وكي لا تتسخ حبال الغسيل بفضلاتك

God on the throne
you try to fix your wings
you are here
learning another lesson
of what you've missed
from the actions of birds
and what is left of dry feather
untouched by water for so long.
God on the throne
depriving you of flying so you would not soar
over the roofs of unfamiliar cities, unlike these…
keeping the clotheslines clean of your waste

يقال بأنك تملك أملاً في أن تفلح بالطيران

وتتحدى العرش

وتنفُضَ وضوء الغيمِ

وتخالف تشريعات الخلق

وما قسم الله لباقي الطير بأن تفعل...

الله على العرش...

يرزق كل ذوات الريش

تروح بطاناً

وأنت تحاول أن تغدو

من مخمصة كي تجمع ما يتسنى

مما استقذره الناس

لكي تتعطر برذاذ الجيفِ الملقاةِ على مرمى بصرك

They say you are hoping to fly
challenging the throne
desecrating the clouds
violating the laws of creation
and God's destiny for birds…
God on the throne
blessing the feathered ones
to return full-stomached
while you try to overcome
hunger and collect leftovers.
You perfume yourself in drizzles of
flesh thrown in the direction of your sight

طعنوا في نَسَبِكَ للبين
وباعوا حُلكتك لصالح كل ضحايا الجوع.
الله على العرش
وأنت على عُكّازين
تحاول تثبيتَ سوادك في الظلمة
كي لا تضلَّ الطريق.
وأنت كما... أنت
تجتثُّ بثورَ الشمس
وتحلم ثانيةً بالطيران

They defamed your ancestry
and sacrificed your darkness for the victims of hunger.
God on the throne,
while you are on crutches
trying to hold down your blackness in the dark
so you don't lose your way.
It is as if you are
holding onto the sun's reins
and dreaming again of flying

نَعيبُك محسوبٌ
ضمن المفقودات لدى قائمةِ الليل
وعكازاك الهرمان
سيحلو للخيبةِ تزيينهما
والنقش على ماء خيالك...
كي يبدو أكثرَ بهرجة مما كان...
وأنت على ذمة بحرٍ...
تقاوم غرق جناحيك.

Your voice is counted
among what's missing on the list of night.
Your aging crutches
dressed in failure
drawing on the water of your imagination
so they would appear fancier than they used to.
Tied up to a sea
your wings resist drowning.

الله على العرش

وأنت تلطّخُ بنعيبك

سكنات الليل

وتبحثُ عن ضوءٍ يبرز حلكتك

لكي تتباهى بالبين

وتعيد لآلهة النحس

هيبتها المفقودة

God sits on the throne
as you stain the stillness of night with your voice
looking for a light to exhibit your darkness
preaching the most evident
and bringing the gods of misfortune
their ever-lost pride

عاجزٌ عن الطيران

كأنك قطعة فحمٍ مبتلة

منفيٌّ عن سربك

مسلوبٌ حلكتك

وموسومٌ بترنح ساقيك

كصاريةٍ تتمسّكُ بالبرق لئلا تسقط.

الله على العرش

يُلقي بجناحيك

إلى أفواهِ الناس

لكي يِسموك بطيرتهم

ولكي يِستعيذوا منك بكلماته التامات

وآياته.... الــ.. أنت منها...

وأنت كما تستحسن

أن تفقأ عبثاً كيسَ مرارتك

لكي تنتقم

وتتلو ما تيسرَ من النعيب

على أسلاكِ الجهد العالي

You are incapable of flying,
like a wet piece of coal -
exiled from your flock,
stripped of your darkness,
marked by your swinging legs;
a mast holding onto lightning not to fall.
God on the throne
feeds your wings
to the mouths of people
casting their spell on you.
They seek protection in his perfect words
and creatures… one of whom you are.
For revenge
you take pleasure in your pain—
singing, with what is left of your voice,
on the high wires of effort.

كنت تنازع شيئاً يزعمه الأسود

في ريشك... في حلكتك

وفي تسبيحك باسم الليل

وباسم الآياتِ المنفياتِ من الذّكرِ

وباسم البين الممنوع من الصرفِ

وباسم العرش الأعظم

كي تثبت أن الليل سيحميك

من اللمعان الخادع حين تنقب عنه

لدى ما استتر وراء ظلامِ الأزقّةِ

ومكبات النفايات... وبعض المتيسر

من سقط متاع العشاق وراء الشرفات

You were fighting a claim
invoked by the blackness of your feather, of your darkness
of your prayers for the night,
for the exiled verses,
and the prohibited logic
and the grand throne
to prove that the night would protect you
from the deceitful glow you're searching for
in the hidden alleys of darkness,
in the garbage dumps,
or in what the lovers left
behind the balconies

وأنت... كما... أنت... كما...

كنت

كما ترغب...

فوق الأسلاك... تبحث عن شؤمٍ

تنقل عدواه وتجمع حفنة نعباتٍ

لتقتل ما بقي من الوقت أمامك

كي تصلح عكازيك

وتمضي.

حيث يكون مكانك لونٌ مألوفٌ عند العطارين

وهواة الشعوذة... وأصحاب اللغة المشبوهة.

حيث تكون... كما أنت

كما... كنت...

تحلّق في سماء الله

وتلهج بالتسبيح المبهم

بين يديّ العرش.

and you are.... as you are
were
as you wish....
standing on the wires… looking for a bad omen
to infect others with cries,
to kill what's left of the time ahead,
to fix your crutches and go on.
To be of familiar color to the healers
and the witchcraft amateurs and the speakers of foul language.
Wherever you are… you are;
however… you were
flying in the sky of god,
mumbling your prayers feverishly
in the hands of the throne.

شكل آخر للقلب

اقرعْ الجرس...
وانفُض شتاءَكَ عن أغنيتك الحزينة
الشريط يُعيدُ نفسه... وجهازُ التسجيل لا يتأثر
بالبرودة!
"My Funny Valentine" يعود
القديسُ المصاب بسهمٍ في القلب يغني
القديسُ يغني ويدعو...
الله يحفظنا... من كل سوء
الله يحبنا... الله يبتلينا... ويبلونا... ويحاسبنا...
ويعاقبنا ويعفو عنا أحياناً.
اللهم اعفُ عني وعن... كل النساء جميعاً
وعن العشّاق جميعاً!

A HEART OF A DIFFERENT SHAPE

Ring the bell
Dust off your winter of that sad song
the recording repeats itself and the recorder does not feel
the cold!
"My Funny Valentine" returns
the heart-wounded saint is singing
singing and praying
that God would protect us all from harm....
God loves us, God afflicts us, troubles us, tries us,
punishes us and sometimes he pardons us.
May he pardon me… and all women
and all lovers!

قالوا قديماً... ليس قديماً جداً

بأن الحب يتخذ شكل القلب الذي يُسكبُ فيه

الحب سائل يتبخر!

الحب سائل... يتجمد!

الحب... له درجة الغليان!

وخُلق القلب وعاءً

له شكل شبه مثلث... أو كما اتفق العشاق على تشكيله

أما قلبي فليس مثلثاً ولا شبه مثلث...

قلبي سائل...

يتخذُ شكل الحب... وشكل الهذيان... وشكل الخوف الذي يسكب فيه

قلبي لا يغلي... ولا يتأثر بأكثر أحوال الطقس رداءة

قلبي سائلٌ عند الحاجة فقط!

"My Funny Valentine" يعود ليبارك وحدتي

فقلبي سائلٌ عندما يحب... ويوضع عادة

في إناء مثقوب!

They said in the old days, not the very old days though,
that love takes the shape of the heart it is poured into
love is an evaporating liquid!
love is a freezing liquid!
love has a boiling point!
and the heart was created as a container
like a semi-perimeter… or in whatever shape lovers have imagined it
But my heart is not a triangle nor a semi-perimeter
my heart is liquid
that takes the shape of love and hallucination,
the shape of fear poured into it
my heart does not boil… nor is it afflicted with bad weather
my heart is liquid only when necessary!
"My funny valentine" returns to bless my solitude
for my heart is liquid when it wishes to be...
usually poured into a holed container!

ها أنتِ... تُعيدين احتواء قلبي السائل
ويتسرب ثانيةً من إنائك المثقوب.
ها هو قلبي مسكوب... ينتظرُ طلوع الشمس ليتبخر!
"My Funny Valentine" يأتي دائماً في الشتاء
حيث لا شمس تكفي لتبخر قلبي.
فليتجمد إذاً... حتى يحين الربيع!
أو حتى تستخدمي جهاز تدفئة مناسب...
يحفظ سيولته... ليبلل قدميك!

Here you are... once again containing my fluid heart,
leaking down from your holed container.
Here is my poured heart... waiting for the sunrise to evaporate!
"My funny valentine" always comes in winter
when no sun is enough to evaporate my heart.
Let it freeze then... until spring!
or you can even use a heater
to keep its liquidity... and wet your feet!

هل أتيتُ في وقتٍ مناسب؟

كي أنسكبَ في انائكِ المثقوب لهذا العام؟

فمن الممتع أن أتخذ شكلكِ ولو للحظات.

من الممتع أن يسري قلبي في عروقكِ بعض الشيء...

وتمنحك اللعنة... التي سكبَتني فيكِ لأول مرة...

"My funny valentine" طويلٌ جداً....

ومملٌ جداً... ووحيدٌ مثلي.

وحيدٌ ثانيةٌ... كالمعتاد!

وحيدٌ جداً... مثل الفالنتين السابق.

did I arrive at the right time?
to be poured into your holed container this year?
it would be a joy to take your shape, even for seconds.
it would be a joy if your heart runs in my veins for a bit
granting you the spell, which had initially poured me into you.
"My funny valentine" is very long
very boring and very lonely like me.
lonely again… as usual!
very lonely… like the one before.

مشهد

رجلٌ وامرأةٌ ترتدي عباءة شرعية يقفان على سفحِ
الجبل
غراب يراقبهما من السماء وكأنه يرى نفسه في
المرآة برفقة رجلٍ لا يحبه...
رجلٌ لا يعرف أن (ابن فرناس) كان نُكتةً تاريخية...
لا يضحك منها سوى غراب ليس مضطراً
لأن يحلم بالطيرانْ!

A SCENE

A man
and a woman in an Islamic cloak
stand on a piedmont.
A crow watches them from the sky
as if seeing himself in a mirror
with a man he doesn't love...
a man who doesn't realize that Ibn Firnas was a joke of history-
only funny enough for a crow that doesn't dream of flying!

أمنيستي

تفويض بالتحقيق مع الحرب
لارتكابها جرائم في حقّ السلاح
والتسبب في اعوجاجِ التاريخ قليلاً... جداً.

AMNESTY

Here's permission to investigate war
for committing crimes against arms
and causing a very slight curve in history

سقط اليوم... ٢٢ قتلى... قتيلاً... حسناً... إنسان/أ
١٨٠ آيلون/ات للسقوط!

Today… 22 dead… okay… 22 humans…
and another 180 are likely to fall!

وفي.......،........ أين وضعت دواء الكحة؟
فلاشات هنا وهناك... يُرجى ضبطُ التعريض
إياك و... أن تنظر للــ الكاميرا!!!

Sudden trouble with the microphone
and with… where did you put the cough syrup?
Flash lights here and there… fix it up
watch out for the… look at the camera!

سأحادثك قريباً...

بعد قليلٍ....... جداً

فأنا لم أرها منذ تعاهدنا ألّا نتبادلَ الخيانة.

I will talk to you soon
very... soon
I haven't seen her since we promised not to betray each other.

بائع السجائر... أغلقَت كُشكَهُ البلدية...

لكنني لا أملك ما يكفي للشراء من آخر...

عربةُ النقل المباشر قريبة....

-شاهد عيان... أنا؟

-هل لديك سيجارة؟

-لقد أغلقت البلدية كشكَ أحمد عبد الغفور

-ولم أنتبه كم من الدبابات مرت من هنا...

- على الأقل... قبل قليل!

-تلك الجميلة هناك... قد تجدون لديها جواباً

the cigarette stand was shut down by the municipality
and I don't have enough to buy from someone else
transportation is close by…
- Me? A witness?
- Do you have a cigarette?
the municipality shut down Ahmed Abdulghafour's stand
and I didn't notice how many tanks passed by
at least… in the last few minutes!
That pretty lady over there… might have an answer for you

...هذا أمر لا ينبغي السكوت عنه...

.

.

.

.

.

.

.

ارتفاع عدد جرائم الحرب...
وتجاهلها لمكالماتي...
والمخالفات التي حررت بحقّ سائق التاكسي
وتحليق البعوض ليلاً

We cannot remain silent about this subject
.
.
.
.
.
.

an increase in the numbers of warcrimes
and the phone calls she ignores
and the tickets issued to the taxi driver
and the mosquitos flying at night

وزكام الزواحف
والتهاب الخياشيم لدى الأسماك
وحساسية البرمائيات
التفاصيل:........................
هذيانٌ مألوف... مثل (براشيمك)
عندما كنت تجتاز الامتحان

bird flu
reptile cold
inflammation of the gills
amphibia allergies
details: ....
this hallucination is familiar… like the cheatsheets you carry
to pass an exam

عفواً... لا تبصقْ أمام واجهةِ المحل
حفاظاً على الصورة الحضارية لمدينتك / نا
ولا أمام قسمِ الشّرطةِ
أو في الأماكن العامة
لكن....
الوقاية خيرٌ من العلاج

Excuse me. do not spit at the shopfront
keep up the civilized image of our/your city
and the police station
and public places.
Prevention is better than cure

إعلانٌ عن......

وظيفة شاغرة...

وإغلاق مصنع...

واحتراق حظيرة أغنام.

نفت الجهات الرسمية...

أن تكون هناك أزمة في المياه

والأمنيسيتي تطالب بالتحقيق

في ارتفاع منسوب الجرائم

وعدد المعتقلين... والأسرى.

الرائحة الكريهة... تعمّ المكان

وشيءٌ من الهدووووووووووء

وبعض الأغاني القديمة

An advertisement for
a vacant job,
a factory shut down,
an animal farm on fire.
officials deny
the water crisis
and Amnesty demands an investigation
following the increase of crime rates
and detainees and prisoners.
the awful smell… surrounds the place
with a bit of quuuuuuietness
and old songs

اشتاقوا لقهوةِ الصباح...

اشتاقوا... والندم على أطراف المدينة

وانبعثت منهم رائحة الصدأ

وتمتماتُ لا معنى لها

والوحشة ينفثها أنفي...

أستنشقها

أستنشقها

أستنشقها....................

....

You must miss the smell of morning coffee
you must miss it… as regret stands on the edges of the city.
A rusty smell rises there
mumbling
I breathe out the longing
and in
in
and in

وفدٌ جديد... وفريق استشاري......

ولجنة / لجنتان

الأمنيسيتي ثانية

a new delegation.... a new team of experts
a committee / two committees
Amnesty again

تحت خطِ الصمت
البعوض مزعجٌ للغاية
وكأنه يُهرّب النوم من زنزانتك
فأسلوبك في النوم انتهاك صارخ...
لاتفاقيات جنيف ... والمواثيق الدولية

Under the line of silence
very annoying mosquitos
steal the sleep from your cell.
Your way of sleeping is an outrageous violation
to the Geneva treaties and international agreements

الهاتف المطلوب... مغلقٌ حالياً
ولا توجد رسائل جديدة
لكنك تملك علبة سجائر جديدة
وزجاجة آيلة للانتهاء
"لولا الهوى... لم تُرِق دمعاً على طللٍ... ولا أرقتَ
لذكر البان والعَلَمِ"
انقطاع التيار الكهربائي وارد....

the number you had dialed… is unavailable now
you got no new messages
but you have a new pack of cigarettes
which you're about to finish.

"Had it not been for the love, you would not have shed tears at the ruins of your beloved /
Nor would you become restless at the remembrance of the cypress and the high mountain"
the electricity could go off any moment…

اضبط نفسك... فلا يمكنك أن تتبول هنا
ارقص بعضَ الشيء
وتقافز وانتهك الآن وقارَ المأتم
القهوة أيضاً .... من مدرّات البول!

Hold yourself together… you can't pee here
dance a bit
Jump around and disturb the reverence of the funeral.
Coffee too… becomes urine!

بالأمسِ هنا...

هنا........

هنا... بالضبطِ!

كان بيتاً...

(تقرير جديد)

Yesterday here…
Here…
Here…exactly!
There was a house…
(a new report)

على الجدران... تتسلى بقراءتها

حتى يحين أوانُ قراءتك الجسد المشبوق

...

...

لا صوت يعلو.......

لا صوت يعلو... فوق صوت الشعب...

لكنك لن تسمع شيئاً

قبل قليل اختُرِق جدارُ الصوت

على الأقل لن يُزعجني البعوض.

on the walls… you enjoy reading
until the time comes for you to read a lusty body
...
...
no voice is stronger
no voice is stronger… than the voice of people
but you cannot hear anything
moments ago the sound barrier was hit
so at least you don't have to worry about the mosquitos anymore

أغنيات قليلة... تتكفل بإعادتك إلى دائرة الإرسال
وإزالة هذيانك... كي تشرب كأساً اخرى
وعلى الأرصفة... ستذكر... كيف
ترَنّحْتَ... أمام الشبّاك المغلق
لكي تستأذن... أن تدخل

a few songs… can take you back to the network range
to get rid of your hallucinations… to drink another glass
on the sidewalks… you will recall how
you stumbled in front of the closed window
for permission… to enter

اصفعيني.......
كي أتمكن من توفيرِ الهذيان
إلى ما بعد رحيلي...

slap me
so I can save my hallucinations
for my departure

وحين يكون هناك وقتٌ
ليحاسبك الوقت... ستدعو ثبوراً
وستَصّلَي... ما قد ضيعت أمام مدافن قصصٍ
لازلت تكابر مدعياً أنك بطلها الأوحد
وحدك......
بطلُ... الــــــ أزقّة
حين تراقب عربات النفايات... تمر أمامك
كالوقت......
كسيجارتك المرتعشة...
كعينيك الحمراوين
كمعطفك المبتل بعَرَقِ بنات الليل
كخطاب محامٍ في لاهاي.

when there's time
to investigate time… you'll pray hard
for what you wasted in the cemeteries of stories
you still think you are her only hero
alone…
hero… of the alleys
when you watch over the dumps… passing in front of you
like time…
like your shivering cigarette
like your red eyes
and the jacket soaked in the sweat of hookers
and the speech of a lawyer in the Hague.

ابتعدوا... كفوا عن التجمهرِ حول العدسات
لدينا عمل لنقوم به...
كي نضمن للإنسان
حياةً أفضل!!

stay away… stop gathering in front of cameras
we have work to do
to guarantee a better life
for humanity!

آخر سلالات اللاجئين

تُصيبُ العالمَ بعسر الهضم... وبعض المشاكل الأخرى!
لا تُجبرِ الأرض على التقيؤ...
وابق قريباً منها... جداً.
كسرٌ غير قابل للجبر...
ولا للإضافة مع أرقام أخرى
فأنت تسبب بعض الارتباك في الإحصاءات الدولية

THE LAST OF THE LINE OF REFUGEE DESCENDANTS
TRANS. JONATHAN WRIGHT

You give the world indigestion, and other problems, too.
Don't force the ground to vomit,
and stay close to it, very close.
A fracture that can't be set,
A fraction that can't be resolved
or added to the other numbers,
You cause some confusion in global statistics.

اللجوء: أن تقف في آخرِ الصف...

كي تحصل على كِسْرِةٍ وطن.

الوقوف: شيئٌ كان يفعله جدك... دون معرفة السبب!

والكسرة: أنت!

الوطن: بطاقةٌ توضع في محفظةِ النقود.

والنقود: أوراق ترسم عليها صور الزعماء.

والصورة: تنوب عنك ريثما تعود.

والعودة: كائن أسطوري... ورد في حكايات الجدة.

انتهى الدرس الأول.

انتقل إليك لكي تتعلم الدرس الثاني: ماذا... معناك؟؟

Being a refugee means standing at the end of the line
to get a fraction of a country.
Standing is something your grandfather did, without knowing the reason.
And the fraction is you.
Country: a card you put in your wallet with your money.
Money: pieces of paper with pictures of leaders.
Pictures: they stand in for you until you return.
Return: a mythical creature that appears in your grandfather's stories.
Here endeth the first lesson.
The lesson is conveyed to you so that you can learn the second lesson, which is
"what do you signify?"

في يوم الحشر... يقفون عراة.
وأنتم تسبحون في ما تصدّع من أنابيبِ الصرفِ الصحي.
حفاةٌ... هذا صحّي للقدمين
لكنه غير صحي للأرض...

On the Day of Judgment, they stand naked,
and you swim in the spillage from the cracked sewage pipes.
Barefoot – that's healthy for the feet
but unhealthy for the ground.

من أجلكم سنقيم المنابرَ... والمؤتمرات.

وستكتب عنكم الصحفُ بشكل لائق.

تم تطوير تركيبة جديدة... للقضاء على الأوساخ المستعصية وبنصف السعر فقط.

سارعوا للحصول على نصف الكمية.

فأزمة المياه حادةٌ جداً.

For your sake we will set up rostrums and hold conferences,
and the newspapers will write about you in the appropriate manner.
A new formula has been developed to eliminate recalcitrant dirt,
and at only half the price.
Hurry to buy up half the amount,
for the water shortage is very acute.

مفاوضات جادة...
تجري لتأمين الرماد مجاناً... كي لا تصاب بالاختناق
دون المساس بحق الأشجار في الحياة على الأرض.
تعلّم ألا تستهلك الرمادَ المخصّص لك...دفعةً واحدة.

Serious negotiations
are underway to provide ashes free of cost so you wouldn't choke,
without affecting the right of trees to live on Earth.
Learn how to avoid using up all your ash allowance in one go.

علَّموك أن ترفع رأسك...
كي لا تشاهدَ الأوساخ على الأرض.
علَّموك أن أمك الأرض
وأبوك؟
تبحث عنه لكي تُثبتَ نَسَبك.
علَّموك أن دموعك إسرافٌ في استهلاكِ الماء
والماء... كما تعلم!

They taught you how to lift your head up
so that you can't see the dirt on the ground.
They taught you that your mother is the Earth.
And your father?
You're looking for him to confirm your lineage.
They taught you that your tears are an extravagant waste of water.
And water ... as you know!

الغد...
يستحسن أن يَتخلَّص منك.
فبدونك شكل الأرض سيصبح أفضل!

Tomorrow,
It'll be a good idea to get rid of you,
because the Earth would look better without you.

الأطفال عصافير...

لكنها... لا تبني أعشاشاً في الأشجار الميتة.

والـمـفـوضـيـة الـعـلـيـا... ليست مسؤولةً عن غرسِ الأشجار.

Children are like sparrows,
but they don't build nests in dead trees.
And the U.N. agency isn't responsible for planting trees.

استخدم نفْسك... ورقة ضغط
ورقة شِعرٍ... ورقة مرحاضٍ
ورقةً كي تشعل أمك نار التنور
وتخبز بضعة أرغفةٍ.

Use yourself as a bargaining card,
as a piece of paper with a poem on it, a piece of toilet paper,
a piece of paper for your mother to light the stove
and bake some loaves.

توقّعات الطقس:
الشمسُ ترقد في الفراشِ لأن حرارتها مرتفعة!

The weather forecast:
The sun is lying in bed because it has a temperature.

العظام... ويكسوها اللحم... ومن ثم الجلد
يتسخ الجلد... ويصدر رائحةً كريهة
يحترق الجلد ويتأثر بالعوامل الخارقة للطبيعة
خذ أنت مثالاً!

The bones are clothed first in flesh and then with skin.
The skin gets dirty and gives off a horrible smell.
The skin burns and is affected by supernatural factors.
Take yourself as an example.

لا تقنطوا...
أبشروا بالغربة التي منها تفرون!
تلك تدريبات مكثفة على العيش في جهنم...
وظروفها القاسية
إلهي... هل جهنّم في مكانٍ ما على الأرض؟

Don't despair.
Take heart in the exile from which you are fleeing!
This is intensive training for the life in Hell
and its harsh conditions.
My god, is Hell somewhere on Earth?

الأنبياء تقاعدوا...
فلا تنتظروا نبياً يبعث لكم... ومن أجلكم
من أجلكم يقدم المراقبون تقاريرَ يومية
ويتقاضون أجوراً عاليةً
كم هو المال ضروريٌّ
من أجل حياة كريمة!

The prophets have gone into retirement
so don't expect one to come and save you.
For your sake the observers submit daily reports
taking home high salaries.
How important money is
to live a decent life!

فلافل أبو سعيد... معرّضةٌ للتلوث
والمستوصف يعلن انتهاء حملة التطعيمات
فلا تخش على أطفالك من التلوث...
مادام المستوصف موجوداً

Abu Said's falafel are exposed to contamination
and the dispensary announced an end to its campaign for vaccinations,
so don't worry about your children being contaminated
as long as the dispensary is there.

نقل حي لوقائع حفل ملكات الجمال

"البكيني" جميل على هذه الفتاة

وتلك أردافها كبيرة بعض الشيء

خبر عاجل " ارتفاع مفاجئ في عدد الوفيات...

بسبب التدخين"

الشمس لا تز ال مصدراً للضوء

والنجوم تتلصّصُ عليك... فسقف منزلك بحاجة

للترميم

Live coverage of the proceedings of the beauty contest:
That girl looks good in her bikini,
that one has rather big hips.
Breaking news: Sudden Rise in the Number of Deaths
from Smoking.
The sun is still a source of light
and the stars are peeping in at you, because your roof needs
repairing.

شجار عند الكراج...

- لم تبلغ السيارة نصابها كي ننطلق

- لكن زوجتي تمر بالمخاض

- هذه الولادة العاشرة لها... ألم تكتسب بعض الخبرة؟

تحذّر التقارير من النمو السكاني العشوائي...

عشوائي... تلك الكلمة التي أبحث عنها منذ زمن!

نحن نعيش في عالم عشوائي!

نحن ننمو بكثرة ويقف أطفالنا عراة...

مصادر إلهام لصنّاع السينما... ولنشرات الأخبار...

وزيارات الوفود... وللنقاش على طاولة الثمانية

الكبار... نحن الصغار... لا يستطيعون العيش بدوننا

من أجلنا... سقطت بعض المباني وانفجرت بعض محطات السكة الحديدية -   الحديد

يتعرض للصدأ

من أجلنا... تكثر الرسائل المصورة

An argument at the taxi depot:
"We don't have enough passengers to leave yet."
"But my wife is in labour."

This is her tenth pregnancy. Hasn't she learnt anything? There are reports warning of random population growth. Random – that's the word I've been looking for for ages. We're living in a random world. We're multiplying and our children stand naked. Sources of inspiration for film-makers, or for discussion around the table at the G8. We are small people but they can't live without us. For our sake some buildings have fallen down and some railway stations have been blown up. Iron is liable to rust. For our sake there are plenty of picture messages

نحن ممثلون بلا أجر نتقاضاه...

دورنا... أن نقفَ عراةً كما ولدَتنا أمهاتنا... كما ولدَتنا الأرض... كما ولدَتنا نشراتُ الأخبار...

والتقارير متعددة الصفحات... والقرى المتاخمة للمستوطنات والمفاتيح التي يحملها جدي...

مسكين جدي

لم يكن يعرف أن الأقفال تغيرت!

جدي... فلتلعنك الأبوابُ التي تفتح بالبطاقات الرقمية... ولتلعنك مياهُ الصرفِ الصحي التي

تمر بجوار قبرك... ولتلعنك السماء فلا تمطر... لا بأس... فعظامك لا يمكنها أن تنبت من تحت

التراب... التراب إذاً هو السبب في عدم نمونا ثانية

جدي... سأقف في يوم الحشرِ نيابة عنك... فعورتي ليست غريبة على الكاميرا...

هل يسمحون بالتصويرِ في يوم الحشر؟!!؟؟

we are actors without getting paid. Our role is to stand as naked as when our mothers gave birth to us, as when the Earth gave birth to us, as the news bulletins gave birth to us, and the multi-page reports, and the villages that border on settlements, and the keys my grandfather carries. My poor grandfather, he didn't know that the locks had changed. My grandfather, may the doors that open with digital cards curse you and may the sewage water that runs past your grave curse you. May the sky curse you, and not rain. Never mind, your bones can't grow from under the soil, so the soil is the reason we don't grow again.

Granddad, I'll stand in for you on the Day of Judgment, because my private parts are no strangers to the camera.
Do they allow filming on the Day of Judgment??!!

جدي... أقف عارياً كل يوم دون حشر... ودون أن يضطر أحد للنفخ في الصور... فأنا مبعوث سلفاً
أنا تجربة الجحيم على كوكب الأرض!
الأرض...
جهنم التي أُعِدّت لل... لاجئين!

Granddad, I stand naked every day without any judgment, without anyone needing to blow any last trumpet, because I have been sent on in advance. I am Hell's experiment on planet Earth.

The Hell that has been prepared for refugees.

أحياناً يكون الحب مثل إفطار صائم!
أحياناً أخرى مثل حذاء رياضي جديد يهدى
لطفل مقعد!
الحب - في الغالب - صفقة تعود بالكثير من
الخسائر..
على جميع الأطراف.

CONCLUSIONS

Sometimes love is like a meal for someone who's been fasting.
At other times it's like new sneakers, given
to a crippled child.
Love, in general, is a deal that brings much loss
to all parties.

INSTRUCTIONS WITHIN

التعليمات بالداخل

NOTES AND COMMENTARY

أشرف فياض
ASHRAF FAYADH

BIO

Ashraf Fayadh is a Palestinian artist and poet born in Saudi Arabia in 1980. He attended Al-Azhar University in Gaza City in 2001, and has been active in the art scene in Saudi Arabia with organizations like Edge of Arabia, a British- Arabian art collaboration. Ashraf also curated exhibitions of Saudi art during Jeddah Art week in Saudi Arabia and in Europe at the 55th Venice Biennale, where he showcased the work of emerging Saudi artists.

CASE

In 2013 Ashraf Fayadh was first detained by Saudi religious police after a disagreement at a cafe, after which he was released on bail; he was then rearrested and tried in 2014. The original verdict was for four years in prison and 800 lashes, but after a secondary appeal he was sentenced to death with the charge of apostasy (heresy) in November of 2015, in keeping with Saudi Arabia's strict adherence to the ultra conservative Wahhabi interpretation of Sharia Islamic Law, within which religious crimes such as blasphemy and apostasy incur the death penalty. The conviction was made on the basis of a prosecution witness who claimed to have heard him blaspheming God, the Prophet Mohammed, and Saudi Arabia, and also on the contents of this book. The testimony of defense witnesses for Fayadh was deemed inadmissable. After an appeal by Fayadh's lawyer, the death sentence was overturned in February of 2016, imposing an eight year prison sentence and 800 lashes , and public repentence through sanctioned media channels.

Since Fayadh's original sentencing, writers, artists and other concerned citizens around the world have appealed for his release, and more than 60 international arts and human rights groups have been active in campaigning on his behalf, calling on both Saudi authorities and Western governmental bodies to seek justice for his case. A worldwide reading was held to gain visibility and support for his case on January 14, 2016, followed by a global "day of creativity" for Ashraf on July 28.

We are grateful to have been able to be in touch with Ashraf after his sentence was lessened, and take heart in his pleasure at this book's release. Wanting to support him in whatever way possible, from this project's inception The Operating System has been dedicated to giving all proceeds from the project to English PEN, an early and consistent advocate, on his behalf, and at his request. PEN will be redistributing this book both in print and ebook formats for the UK Market, and is committed to continuing to fight on his behalf.

- The Operating System

CONTRIBUTORS AND COLLABORATORS

MONA KAREEM (translation lead) *is a poet, translator, and journalist based in New York. She is the author of three poetry collections, some of which were translated into French, English, Spanish, Dutch, German, Farsi, Italian and Kurdish. Mona is a doctoral candidate in the Comparative Literature program at Binghamton University. Her dissertation explores issues of subalternity in the Arab feminist novel. She teaches writing classes while freelancing for a number of Arabic publications.*

JONATHAN WRIGHT (translation) *is a British literary translator who specializes in translating contemporary Arabic fiction into English. He turned to literary translation after 30 years as a journalist, mainly in the Middle East with the London-based news agency Reuters, based in Egypt, Sudan, Lebanon, Oman, Tunis and Cyprus. Since 2008 he had translated more than a dozen novels and collections of short stories and essays, including works by Alaa al-Aswany, Youssef Ziedan, Hassan Blasim, Rasha al Ameer, Galal Amin and Saud Alsanoussi. He won the Banipal Prize for Arabic Literary Translation in 2013 for his translation of Youssef Ziedan's Azazeel and shared the Independent Foreign Fiction Prize in 2014 with author Hassan Blasim for Blasim's The Iraqi Christ. He studied Arabic as an undergraduate at St. John's College, Oxford.*

MONA ZAKI (translation) *earned her Ph.D. from Princeton University in medieval Islamic history. She is a translator and reviewer of modern Arabic fiction and currently teaches in the Dept. of Modern Languages and Literature at the College of William and Mary in Virginia. She is a contributing editor of Banipal.*

AMMIEL ALCALAY (translation editor) *is a poet, novelist, translator, critic, and scholar, whose books include* After Jews and Arabs, Memories of Our Future, Islanders, *and* neither wit nor gold: from then. *Translations include* Sarajevo Blues *and* Nine Alexandrias *by Bosnian poet Semezdin Mehmedinović; he has also published translations from Arabic, French, Hebrew, Italian, and Latin. Recent work includes a 10th anniversary edition of* from the warring factions *(with an introduction by Diane di Prima), and* a little history, *both out in 2013 from re:public / UpSet. He teaches at Queens College and The Graduate Center, CUNY, and is founder and General Editor of Lost & Found: The CUNY Poetics Document Initiative, a series of student and guest edited archival texts emerging from the New American Poetry.*

PIERRE JORIS (translation editor) *Pierre Joris most recently published* The Agony of I.B. *(a play commissioned & produced in June 2016 by the Théatre National du Luxembourg; Editions PHI);* An American Suite *(early poems; inpatient press 2016); &* Barzakh: Poems 2000-2012 *(Black Widow Press 2014). Recent translations include* Breathturn into Timestead: The Collected Later Poetry of Paul Celan *(FSG) &* The University of California Book of North African Literature *(vol. 4 in the Poems for the Millennium series), coedited with Habib Tengour.*

LYNNE DESILVA-JOHNSON (translation editor, volume editor, design) *is a slinger of image, text, sound, and code, a frequent collaborator across a wide range of disciplines, a community activist, and a regular curator of events in NYC and beyond. She served as an adjunct in the CUNY system for a decade, and as a K-12 teaching artist since 2001. Also a social practice artist and poet, she has appeared at The Dumbo Arts Festival, Naropa University, Bowery Arts and Science, The NYC Poetry Festival, Eyebeam, Undercurrent Projects, Mellow Pages, The New York Public Library, The Poetry Project, Independent Curators International, and the Cooper Union, among others. She is the founder and managing editor of The Operating System, and the libraries editor of Boog City.*

CONTRIBUTORS AND COLLABORATORS

TO ALL OUR TRANSCRIBERS :: A SPECIAL THANK YOU!!!

This volume presented an unexpected hurdle when we discovered quite far along in the process that we were unable to procure a typed document file of Fayadh's original book, which meant that in order to proceed with our plan to produce a complete Arabic-English dual language translation, true to his original version, the entire book had to be transcribed before it could be laid out.

With the help of Ammiel Alcalay, who then enlisted Mohamad Hodeib, who in turn enlisted the following roster of kind and generous souls, based in Beirut -- a team that sprang into action distributing and diligently copying out sections of the book manually. We quickly had the Arabic in hand, well in time to be laid out and go to press on schedule. It could not have happened without them!

KAMELLA LAKKIS - Graduate Student at Lebanese Conservatory / University
FARAH ARIDI - Word enthusiast from Lebanon. Teaches English Literature and Culture Studies. PhD student of Comparative Literature at Goldsmiths University, London.
KHALED AL HILLI - PhD Candidate in Comparative Literature at the Graduate Center, CUNY
HASSAN HARB - Doctoral Student in Quantum Chemistry, University of California Merced
NOUR CHOUMAN - Public Health Officer, Universite St-Joseph de Beyrouth, Medical Student
MOWAFAK ALLAHAM

MOHAMAD J HODEIB (Walad) is a writer, researcher, and cultural activist. Born and raised in Beirut, he founded el-Yafta literary community (2011) through he organizes writing-related activities, workshops, and poetry readings. Hodeib conceptualized, produced and staged two shows, blending elements of spoken word, music and theatre (Mahrajan al-Shob, 2012 & B'intithar al-Harb al-Qadima, 2013). He published his compilation of Lebanese colloquial poems (Al-Shaware', 2013), and was featured in various art & literary platforms in Beirut and New York, including TEDxLAU (2013), Bowery Poetry Club (2015-16), and the Nuyorican Poets Cafe (2016). He was offered an art residency at Haven for Artists in the summer of 2016 to direct a two-months writers' workshop in Beirut. He is currently completing an MA in Middle East Studies at CUNY, New York.

EL YAFTA is a Beirut-based band of poets and literary circle. Founded in 2011, it organizes a vast array of events and activities corresponding to writing, performance, and the arts. From readings and events, to writers' workshops, it transgresses the boundaries of closed-door collaborations to nurture a network of cultural activists within a collective, creative community that maintains at its core the essentiality of individual self-fulfillment of the artist.

THIS BOOK IS NOT BACKWARDS

Publishing, Proprioception, Politics
and the Hope in Disruption

You hold in your hands, right now, a book that represents so many things — a book which is transgressive in myriad ways you perhaps haven't even begun to consider — but you've likely been intimately aware of its right binding and of the Arabic language running through its pages, language you likely aren't able to read.

To my non-Arabic readers and scholars I ask you: have you ever held an Arabic book in your hands? have you looked at an Arabic newspaper or magazine? Perhaps you've seen Arabic writing in museums, in textbooks, but the likelihood of you owning a document or volume that includes any significant length of Arabic writing is slim to none. Indeed — perhaps picking up this volume even gave you pause?

To have Ashraf Fayadh's *Instructions Within* as the first volume in The Operating System's "Glossarium: Unsilenced Texts" series is fitting — and also an honor. An honor, because Ashraf's voice is singular, searing, and his story so vital to share with the world, at this time and in the future. Fitting, because both the book and Ashraf's case itself demonstrate the potential power of creative output, not only in content but also in his sentencing — as Tahar Ben Jalloun has written,

"*this sentence teaches us all we need to know about his poetry — about his strength, about his violence. Poets are insurgents, carriers of fire, companions of truth and of evidence. They are the light which goes out into the darkness and gives words to things which die from not having been said. They are fragile and strong at the same time. They possess only their breath, their souls, who resist. We can hit them, whip when, throw them to the bottom of a well, bury them alive, but their voices continue to rise, and wake up the world*".

The harshness of punishment in regimes like the current climate of Saudi Arabia, where Ashraf is so clearly, to our sensibility, unjustly imprisoned, has something to teach us: our words carry fire, our art carries regime change in its fist…we are powerful, dangerous, a risk to the powers that be.

With the Unsilenced Texts series my intention is to seek out and encourage, to permit where there has been repression those texts from all corners of the globe, from past and present, that remind us of our shared humanity, texts in which we can find ourselves in the voices and inner lives of others, even as those others at times suffer.

This series is, in many ways, the direction The Operating System has always been headed, even in its nascent beginnings. For even with its English publications, and in its online projects, our mission has always been 'unsilencing' - soliciting and facilitating voices, encouraging an archival sensibility, insisting upon framing and process writing. As an agile experiment, this "unsilencing" began close to home: who wasn't writing, or sharing, or archiving their valuable creative process / vision? What poets avoided the slogging requirements of the current publishing environment, preferring to engage in community projects and/or their own private ongoing writing practice, but could be coaxed out of the woodwork with encouragement?

Unsilencing the self, encouraging the recognition of self-as-maker, granting permission and agency to the maker as valid, teaching skills as viable, this has been the bread and butter of the OS in its first years: ultimately, an activist exercise in modeling what I, as an under-resourced woman without much other than technology, education, and design at my disposal, could do — and therefore, what others were capable of.

It was only after scaling with these local exercises that it felt appropriate to begin to approach the threshold of responsibility vis-a-vis bringing a foreign text into the United States as a publisher here, which I see as a hugely vital task — and privilege, not to be taken lightly. Having achieved distribution of a certain scale, having the titles already in place in order to be assigned Library of Congress cataloguing numbers — these mundanities take time, but they also assure a title like Ashraf's that it will see wide scale availability, potential adoption in classrooms, and perhaps most importantly, a permanent place in the archive.

And, critically — that permanent place in the archive will not only be occupied by the translation of "Instructions Within" but also with the work in its original Arabic, as written by Ashraf himself.

It is no secret that as I write these words, in 2016, this classic, historic and beautiful language, (with origins that date back to the 4th century AD, and which is native to well over 400 million people), is so stigmatized that its readers, speakers and scholars fear for their lives. Readers and speakers of Arabic — Muslim and non-Muslim alike — are routinely the victims of hate crimes, are kicked off of airplanes, are held in detainment, are subject to appalling treatment both officially and socially.

But it is essential that we give back to this language and to its speakers and scholars the respect and recognition they deserve as global citizens, as sentient beings, and as creators possessed of a shared human history. We must actively work to normalize this language across diverse communities -- to engage with its contemporary and historical forms, as part of a larger effort towards a common, translingual experience both in the arts and in lived experience.

Each of The Operating System's books questions design standards in order to dislodge our normative patterning and expectation, with the belief that continuous exposure to diversity on the page — both in content and design — affects not only the cognitive brain but the body as well, in so far as this requires the "rewiring" of brain behaviors, essentially getting us out of a "rut" of repetitive reception.

Instructions Within goes one step farther — requiring the western reader to hold and read the book as one would an Arabic or Hebrew volume, that is, by being right-bound. The westerner might find him or herself saying that the book "starts at the back" or feeling vaguely uncomfortable holding the book and/or turning pages "backwards" but this is precisely the point: to disrupt the proprioceptic modelling that tells you that the way you do things, your patterning, is not only yours but "right" or "normal," when in fact hundreds of millions of people — billions of people — experience books and texts in directions different from our own.

Why does a book go right to left, or left to right? Why is text right aligned or left aligned? It's worth investigating the history of these things, whether you're a writer, a publisher, a designer, or simply a reader — so that you might become connected to, aware of the unwitting behaviors you've collected without intention or question along the way. What I can say, and what I do know, is that I have no preference either way — from a design standpoint, I move text on the page based on negative space, on feeling, on tightness or air, much like one handles visual composition.

But why have Ashraf's book, this translation, right bound, including all the Arabic and not only an excerpt, alongside the translation? It's sad to say that I cannot know if copies of Ashraf's original publication of this text, printed in 2008, will survive - especially in the Arab world, where archives are in such grave danger. Who is to know how many copies were printed, how many made it into global archives or libraries — hopefully more than the one I am aware of. What I know now, through printing this book, in this way, is that Ashraf's title, his name, and his poems all persist not only for English readers but for Arabic readers in the US and all over the world, now and in the future, in the way they were written, the way he as artist and poet intended, becoming more widely available than ever before, and assuring him as best I can that his original work will last well beyond any of our lifetimes, no matter the outcome of his case.

But what of his case, and what are we to do, on a practical level, everyday?

Make art, not war. No, really.

It is clearer than ever that policy makers, politicians, CEO's, and many privileged people are dominated by fear, a fear that is fanned by the culture they have built that is now eating them, their children — and any chance of an earth that will be here for future generations — alive. For those who have played a role in the growth of this disaster, accepting publicly or even internally the scale of the egregious, inhumane behaviors and foibles of post-industrial consumer dominated culture is mind boggling. Psychological collapse for many is close at hand ; all too often the ability to simply keep going is fed by consumption and facilitated by medication of both illegal and prescribed varieties.

The common experience of anger attached to shame and feelings of inadequacy or inability is one that is, and rightfully so, also linked to highly sensitive considerations of privilege; yet, the problem is widespread across all communities, as even top level schools and cultural norms shift away from intellectual, civic, and political literacy to an increasingly hostile, consumer-driven, anti-intellectual environment, in both public and private arenas. Our schools -- driven by numbers and increasingly specialized -- are by and large not producing a critically thinking populace, and we see every day how politicians and propaganda media owned by moneyed interests prey on the fears and confusion of the citizenry.

That said — as a result of this landscape of emotional landmines in a increasingly anti-intellectual context can render a certain type of direct, Euclidean logic an offensive, ineffective, and often counterproductive strategy.

In the classroom I sought to teach my students to see academic and scientific writing, as well as journalism (and other types of public communication) as "codes" — that is, as other languages that without training they should feel no shame in not being able to parse, any more than any other foreign language. However, this perspective is a rare one, and it remains a challenge to speak in a world devoid of this awareness -- to publish, lecture, even to engage in conversation (on or offline) without hitting walls borne of deep discomfort.

A change of tack from the production of "objective" social science and highly rigorous coded discourse to "art," to the production of publications as well as presentations across a range of media that on first take might be considered more "creatively" oriented might seem frivolous, or like a "side project" when one's primary goals are systemic evolution and change but in fact it's just the opposite: it's an alternative approach and a model, for those who come to realize that the way we're communicating is driving us apart.

I have come to believe that it will be through "art": i.e., through the disruption of our sensory perception of eye / ear, through language and ultimately through those things' connection to our emotional bodies that we can wear away at our cognitive conditioning in ways that direct language can no longer achieve for large parts of the population. Add to this the ways in which emotion is inextricably linked to the reasons we're not getting anywhere with argument, and begin to see how emotion (and compassion) in both consciousness and body may be our link back to possibilities, and to (r)evolution.

For the ones of us working for change, what does this mean? Should we not try to talk about what's going on in the world? Should we stay away from facts and figures? From theory? This seems a dangerous course of action as well, if for different reasons.

I don't have the answer, and don't think there is any single solution. However, in your hands you hold an example of the type of project with which we might begin to toe this line: an Arabic-English dual-langauge translation of Ashraf Fayadh's controversial 2008 poetry collection. Add to this the story of how our tiny organization / independent press in Brooklyn NY, came to be publishing the translation of a Palestinian political prisoner in a Saudi prison, and you begin to see the ways in which we, mere drops of water, might begin to wear away the stone.

First and foremost, this book (like all our books) exists because I believed that we could help, and in this case it exists because, not seeing anyone else step up to the plate, I offered, before knowing how we would make it happen. But it also exists because before seeing Ashraf as Palestinian, or as Saudi prisoner, the words of his that I had heard opened my heart to him -- not as a poet, or as an artist, but as a human, and I wept many times to imagine his suffering, and the suffering of others experiencing grave injustice. I say this not to speak of my own experience but rather for what this suggests about the universal response to other sentient beings, when we strip away the trappings of labels and move away from fear borne of unfamiliarity and propaganda. There were few dry eyes at the reading I first attended, and I believe that more than any statistic it is in this very personal, emotional, experience of connection that the seed of change will be sown. And that seed thrives when it lands on both left and right brain: via music, art, performance, or poetry.

Through The Operating System, I have been able to develop a platform to produce and distribute work aligned with this vision — with collaborators like Ashraf, whom even behind bars, and nearly 7000 miles away, I knew immediately as a friend and ally in a struggle bigger and more important than any of our struggles alone. Like Sō Percussion, composers and musicians with whom we're facilitating a volume documenting their many year process of developing and performing "A Gun Show," considering the complex role of the gun in the American Imaginary, which will premiere at BAM this fall. And that's just the beginning.

Crucially, too — while we might be known best for our publishing projects, in fact we are a hub for a wide range of programs which seek to cross pollinate not only between different disciplines within the arts but also within different industries, in the service of peer to peer learning both immediately and in the future, via the development of open source / archival materials; in addition our own process has been transparent from day one, seeking to model possibility for others rather than competing with them.

Of course, while there is still great value in the circulation, publication, and archiving of language in many forms [in journalism, in continued academic and public political and social discourse, and in nonfiction], the current highly manipulated (and manipulating) institutional structures of news media and higher education have left many burned and understandably wary, unable to receive the "instructions within" those books and texts. In this wake of distrust, and looking out at the horizon of emotionally fraught, highly defensive, intellectually and literally warring factions we find both across the US and the world, even the most intelligent arguments can't and won't save us. So until then, we'll keep putting other possibilities into print, and into libraries and archives. For it will, indeed, be the poets (musicians, artists, creators of all kinds) who "wake up the world."

- Lynne DeSilva-Johnson, August 2016

GLOSSARIUM: UNSILENCED TEXTS AND MODERN TRANSLATIONS was established in early 2016 in an effort to recover silenced voices outside and beyond the familiar poetic canon, seeking out and publishing both contemporary translations and little known (and unknown) out of print texts, in particular those under siege by restrictive regimes and silencing practices in their home (or adoptive) countries.

The term "Glossarium" derives from latin/greek and is defined as "a collection of glosses or explanations of words, especially of words not in general use, as those of a dialect, locality or an art or science, or of particular words used by an old or a foreign author." The series is was initiated by and is curated by Managing Editor Lynne DeSilva-Johnson, with the help of contributing editors Ariel Resnikoff and Stephen Ross, as well as a wide range of global allies and friends.

"Instructions Within" is the first book in this important new series, which will be followed later in 2016 and then in 2017 by two Spanish-English translations by Margaret Randall. The first is Gregory Randall's award winning memoir of life in Cuba, *"To Have Been There Then (Estar Allí Entonces),"* originally published in Uruguay to great acclaim in 2010. The second is *"Viaje de Regreso / Return Trip,"* a dual language edition of Cuban poet Israel Dominguez's striking poetry, with a beautiful cover featuring Havana street art by Jose Parla and JR.

Advance Praise for *"To Have Been There Then"*:

"Gregory Randall has done it: written a captivating, ethically humane, and inspirational memoir of growing up in revolutionary Cuba as a child of exiled political activists. He is able to tell forthright yet loving stories of his engaged life with multiple fathers, escaping the 1968 military crackdown in Mexico as a seven year-old in charge of his younger siblings, forging friendships in Cuban boarding schools, and living his adolescence as an intellectual and political coming-of-age banquet among artists and revolutionaries from across the continent. He sees dogma and cant yet remains deeply committed to the vision of a liberated space and new women and men. Read this powerful book and be stirred anew to live fully in harmony with your values." -Bernardine Dohrn

"Gregory Randall grew up in revolutionary Cuba. He left in 1983, and later he and his wife Laura relocated to Uruguay and Gregory established himself within the academic world there. Revolutionary Cuba's literacy campaign in 1960-61, which sent young people into the mountains during a period that included the Bay of Pigs invasion, is generally recognized. Cuba's far flung medical assistance in situations like the recent Haitian earthquake is also well-known. This book explores the more comprehensive Cuban effort to create what the Zapatistas call un otro mundo, another world. I know of no other book that so richly provides an empathetic view of the twentieth-century socialist project from both within and without. —Staughton Lynd

"To Have Been There Then is an extraordinary book. Gregory Randall recreates scenes from a revolutionary childhood and youth in Mexico and Cuba during the 1960s and 70s with brilliant vividness that brings an adult's wisdom to the child's perspective. He evokes the spirit of revolutionary consciousness of the era, when Cuba's radical experimentation and commitment to building a new world intersected with revolutionary dreams and movements throughout Latin America. Randall's childhood was peopled with artists, intellectuals, and revolutionaries from throughout the continent who shared a deep belief in the possibility for radical social change. Cuba's revolutionary history is told here with verve and drama, through personal detail of a child and young man coming of age in truly historic circumstances."
–Aviva Chomsky, author of The Cuban Revolution, co-editor of The Cuba Reader: History, Culture, Politics.

"Here is the perfect book for this time of change in US-Cuban relations, and when a new generation in the United States has embraced the idea and goals of socialism and human solidarity. Gregory Randall's exquisite coming of age story, set in Cuba during the second decade of the Cuban Revolution, is unflinchingly truthful and compassionate." – Roxanne Dunbar-Ortiz, historian and author most recently of An Indigenous Peoples' History of the United States.

Gregory Randall was born in New York City in 1960, then lived eight years in Mexico, fourteen in Cuba, eleven in France and since 1994 has resided in Uruguay. He and his wife have three children and one grandchild. He did his undergraduate work in telecommunications in Cuba and earned his doctorate in information technology from the University of Orsay, France. Since 1994 he has been a professor of electrical engineering at the University of the Republic in Montevideo. From 2007 to 2014 he was also that institution's vice president for research, during which time he promoted and oversaw the establishment of several university campuses in the interior of the country. To Have Been There Then is his first book, a memoir of childhood and young adulthood in the Cuba of the 1970s and '80s, with moving, often breathtaking stories of what it was like for a young boy to grow up in revolution.

Advance Praise for "Return Trip"

"A breathtaking book by a major Cuban poet. Margaret Randall's translations beautifully embody Israel Dominguez's yearning for a future of justice for all. His yearning is his gift to all of us who seek a different way of being in the world. Return Trip is a welcome and necessary poetry."- Demetria Martinez, recipient of an International Latino Book Award and an American Book Award for The Block Captain's Daughter.

"Margaret Randall's clear and lively translation of Viaje de Regreso / Return Trip *invites us into the life and work of a poet born in the early 1970s, nearly 25 years into the Revolution. Domínguez's poems represent the lyric tradition in the best sense; they are poems investigating the emotion of the experience living in one's body, in one's mind. Written from a photograph or a memory, these poems explore love, family, spirituality, material reality. Many of these poems are dedicated to friends, family, mentors, and attest to a relationality and love that's both humbling and inspiring. In these poems of dense image and rich sensation, Randall presents us with the gift of her translation of Israel Domínguez's poetry."* - Stephen Motika

Viaje de Regreso / Return Trip is a compendium of nostalgia, in which a familiar street, an old photograph, or memory of when the trains ran on precision time take up residence in poems in which a mature philosophy of life breaks through a patina of childhood wonder. A clothesline becomes a highway. A plum tree calms the spirit. A public restroom holds a dark menace. A woman's name floats in a swimming pool. A hero of the Great War looms upon the horizon. Through it all, the music and culture of the country to the north refuse to fade into oblivion; despite the ever-present weight of political attack from the United States, a love for its popular culture remains familiar and strong. The poet writes: "Glory belongs to my neighbor / who owns a Buick / and wears a lot of gold."

Israel Domínguez was born in Placetas, Villa Clara, in 1973. Throughout his childhood his father recited poetry, and he and his mother often accompanied him to his performances. By the time Domínguez graduated from the University of Havana in 1996, his family had moved to Matanzas and he joined them there. His work has been awarded numerous prizes. Among his poetry collections are: Hojas de cal (2001), Collage mientras avanza mi carro de equipaje (2002), Sobre un fondo de arena (2004), Después de acompañar a William Jones (2007), and Viaje de regreso (2011). In an interview, he has said: "Memory is a return trip, inherent of course to the human being. In my poetry it is not simply an instrument but also its landscape, that is to say, a poetic event [. . .] It's not a matter of reducing memory to its individual manifestation because collective memory influences the individual and vice versa " Domínguez lives in Matanzas, where he also works as a translator. Like so many others, his professional life has been affected by Cuba's precarious economy; for a number of years, and because he could earn so much more in the tourism sector, he quit a job in his profession to take one as a bellboy at a hotel on Varadero Beach. The experience provided material for a book of poems. Happily, he is once more working in his chosen field.

TITLES IN THE PRINT: DOCUMENT COLLECTION

Death is a Festival - Anis Shivani [2018]

In Corpore Sano : Creative Practice and the Challenged Body [Anthology, 2017]
Lynne DeSilva-Johnson and Jay Besemer, co-editors
Nothing Is Wasted - Shabnam Piryaei [2017]
To Have Been There Then / Estar Alli Entonces - Gregory Randall (trans. Margaret Randall) [2017]
The Color She Gave Gravity - Stephanie Heit [2017]
The Science of Things Familiar - Johnny Damm[Graphic/Poetry Hybrid, 2017]
You Look Something - Jessica Tyner Mehta [2017]
One More Revolution - Andrea Mazzariello [2017]
Flower World Variations, Expanded Edition/Reissue - Jerome Rothenberg and Harold Cohen [2017]
Animal Instinct - Nada Faris [2017]
Return Trip / Viaje Al Regreso ; Spanish-English Dual Language Edition - Israel Dominguez,
(trans. Margaret Randall) [2017]

Instructions Within - Ashraf Fayadh [2016]
Arabic-English dual language edition; Mona Kareem, translator
Let it Die Hungry [2016] - Caits Meissner
A GUN SHOW [2016] - So Percussion in Collaboration with Ain Gordon and Emily Johnson
agon [2016] - Judith Goldman
Everybody's Automat [2016] - Mark Gurarie
How to Survive the Coming Collapse of Civilization [2016] - Sparrow
CHAPBOOK SERIES 2016: OF SOUND MIND
*featuring the quilt drawings of Daphne Taylor
Improper Maps - Alex Crowley; While Listening - Alaina Ferris;
Chords - Peter Longofono; Any Seam or Needlework - Stanford Cheung

TEN FOUR - Poems, Translations, Variations [2015]- Jerome Rothenberg, Ariel Resnikoff, Mikhl Likht
MARILYN [2015] - Amanda Ngoho Reavey
CHAPBOOK SERIES 2015: OF SYSTEMS OF
*featuring original cover art by Emma Steinkraus
Cyclorama - Davy Knittle; The Sensitive Boy Slumber Party Manifesto - Joseph Cuillier;
Neptune Court - Anton Yakovlev; Schema - Anurak Saelow
SAY/MIRROR [2015; 2nd edition 2016] - JP HOWARD

Moons Of Jupiter/Tales From The Schminke Tub [plays, 2014] - Steve Danziger
CHAPBOOK SERIES 2014: BY HAND
Pull, A Ballad - Maryam Parhizkar; Executive Producer Chris Carter - Peter Milne Grenier;
Spooky Action at a Distance - Gregory Crosby; Can You See that Sound - Jeff Musillo

CHAPBOOK SERIES 2013: WOODBLOCK
*featuring original prints from Kevin William Reed
Strange Coherence - Bill Considine;; The Sword of Things - Tony Hoffman;
Talk About Man Proof - Lancelot Runge / John Kropa;
An Admission as a Warning Against the Value of Our Conclusions -Alexis Quinlan

WHY PRINT / DOCUMENT?

The Operating System uses the language "print document" to differentiate from the book-object as part of our mission to distinguish the act of documentation-in-book-FORM from the act of publishing as a backwards facing replication of the book's agentive *role* as it may have appeared the last several centuries of its history. Ultimately, I approach the book as TECHNOLOGY: one of a variety of printed documents (in this case bound) that humans have invented and in turn used to archive and disseminate ideas, beliefs, stories, and other evidence of production.

Ownership and use of printing presses and access to (or restriction of) printed materials has long been a site of struggle, related in many ways to revolutionary activity and the fight for civil rights and free speech all over the world. While (in many countries) the contemporary quotidian landscape has indeed drastically shifted in its access to platforms for sharing information and in the widespread ability to "publish" digitally, even with extremely limited resources, the importance of publication on physical media has not diminished. In fact, this may be the most critical time in recent history for activist groups, artists, and others to insist upon learning, establishing, and encouraging personal and community documentation practices. Hear me out.

With The OS's print endeavors I wanted to open up a conversation about this: the ultimately radical, transgressive act of creating PRINT /DOCUMENTATION in the digital age. It's a question of the archive, and of history: who gets to tell the story, and what evidence of our life, our behaviors, our experiences are we leaving behind? We can know little to nothing about the future into which we're leaving an unprecedentedly digital document trail — but we can be assured that publications, government agencies, museums, schools, and other institutional powers that be will continue to leave BOTH a digital and print version of their production for the official record. Will we?

As a (rogue) anthropologist and long time academic, I can easy pull up many accounts about how lives, behaviors, experiences — how THE STORY of a time or place — was pieced together using the deep study of correspondence, notebooks, and other physical documents which are no longer the norm in many lives and practices. As we move our creative behaviors towards digital note taking, and even audio and video, what can we predict about future technology that is in any way assuring that our stories will be accurately told – or told at all?

As a creative practitioner, the stories, journals, and working notes of other creative practitioners have been enormously important to me. And yet so many creative people of this era no longer put together physical documents of their work – no longer have physical archives of their writing or notebooks, typed from the first draft to the last, on computers. Even visual artists often no longer have non-digital slides and portfolios. How will we leave these things for the record?

How will we say WE WERE HERE, WE EXISTED, WE HAVE A DIFFERENT STORY?

- Lynne DeSilva-Johnson, Founder/Managing Editor,
THE OPERATING SYSTEM, Brooklyn NY 2016

DOC U MENT
/däkyə m ə nt/

First meant "instruction" or "evidence," whether written or not.

noun - a piece of written, printed, or electronic matter that provides information or evidence or that serves as an official record
verb - record (something) in written, photographic, or other form
synonyms - paper - deed - record - writing - act - instrument

[*Middle English, precept, from Old French, from Latin documentum, example, proof, from docre, to teach; see dek- in Indo-European roots.*]

Who is responsible for the manufacture of value?

Based on what supercilious ontology have we landed in a space where we vie against other creative people in vain pursuit of the fleeting credibilities of the scarcity economy, rather than freely collaborating and sharing openly with each other in ecstatic celebration of MAKING?

While we understand and acknowledge the economic pressures and fear-mongering that threatens to dominate and crush the creative impulse, we also believe that now more than ever we have the tools to relinquish agency via cooperative means, fueled by the fires of the Open Source Movement.

Looking out across the invisible vistas of that rhizomatic parallel country we can begin to see our community beyond constraints, in the place where intention meets resilient, proactive, collaborative organization.

Here is a document born of that belief, sown purely of imagination and will. When we document we assert. We print to make real, to reify our being there. When we do so with mindful intention to address our process, to open our work to others, to create beauty in words in space, to respect and acknowledge the strength of the page we now hold physical, a thing in our hand.... we remind ourselves that, like Dorothy: *we had the power all along, my dears.*

THE PRINT! DOCUMENT SERIES
is a project of
the trouble with bartleby

in collaboration with
the operating system